A Plethora of Poetry and Prose

A Plethora of Poetry and Prose

Julie Nancy Wiltshire

Copyright © 2025 Julie Nancy Wiltshire
Illustrations by Maria Over

The moral right of the author has been asserted.

Apart from any fair dealing for the purposes of research or private study, or criticism or review, as permitted under the Copyright, Designs and Patents Act 1988, this publication may only be reproduced, stored or transmitted, in any form or by any means, with the prior permission in writing of the publishers, or in the case of reprographic reproduction in accordance with the terms of licences issued by the Copyright Licensing Agency. Enquiries concerning reproduction outside those terms should be sent to the publishers.

The manufacturer's authorised representative in the EU
for product safety is Authorised Rep Compliance Ltd,
71 Lower Baggot Street, Dublin D02 P593 Ireland (www.arccompliance.com)

Troubador Publishing Ltd
Unit E2 Airfield Business Park,
Harrison Road, Market Harborough,
Leicestershire. LE16 7UL
Tel: 0116 2792299
Email: books@troubador.co.uk
Web: www.troubador.co.uk

ISBN 978-1-83628-329-4

British Library Cataloguing in Publication Data.
A catalogue record for this book is available from the British Library.

Printed and bound by CPI Group (UK) Ltd, Croydon, CR0 4YY
Typeset in 11pt Adobe Garamond Pro by Troubador Publishing Ltd, Leicester, UK

Dedicated to all my family and friends.

Contents

A BRIDGE TOO FAR
A CACOPHONY OF SOUND
A DAY AT THE SEASIDE
A DUSTING OF DEATH
A LEAF IN THE CHAPTER OF WAR
A PEACEFUL SATISFACTION
A SNOWY CHRISTMAS
ABORTION
ADDICTION
AGED MOLE
ALONG THE BRUTAL SHORES OF MY WORLD
AMID THE WINTER SNOW
AN UNWANTED VISITOR
AS THE STARS BLOW OUT OF THE SKY
BEIGE JACKETS
BELLY DANCING IN BIRKENHEAD
BIRD BROOCH
BLINDED BY NORMALITY
BOB
BRIZZLE BLUES

CAMERA CRAZY
CAN I BEGIN ANEW?
CANCER THE CRAB
   (KNOW THYSELF)
COBWEB
CONCRETE COFFIN
COSTA COFFEE
DARK DEEDS
DENT DE LION
DIAMOND IN THE SKY
DON'T WALK IN MY SHOES
ENSANGUINING OUR HEAVY
   HEARTS
ENVIRONMENTAL RAPE
FLY FISHING
FORGIVENESS
FREEDOM OF THE FALL
FUNNEL TO THE FUTURE
GALLOPING TO MY GRAVE
GRANDCHILDREN
HAIR
HELL HATH NO FURY
HIDDEN WITHIN MYSELF
HIDE AND SEEK
HOLDING FATE IN THE PALM OF HER
   HAND

HOROSCOPE
1 AM A DAGLOCK
I WILL NOT BE WINDOW
    DRESSED
I'M SORRY HONEY
IN THE SHALLOWS OF MY SOUL
JOURNEYING INTO THE NIGHT
JUST A DYING LEAF IN THE WIND
KNAPSACK
KOI
LIFE HANGING BY A THREAD
LIMNODYNASTES DORSALIS (THE LORD
    OF THE MARSHES)
LIMPET
LINES OF LONELINESS IN THE SAND
LOVE
MAKING THE CHANGE
SWEET SUSAN
THE BIRD FEEDER
THE BRIEFEST OF SECONDS
THE BRUTA SHORES OF MY WORLD
THE DUTY VISIT
FOOT AND MOUTH
THE FINALITY OF OUR WORLD
THE FIRE OF FATE
THE FROG

THE GHOSTLY TUNE
THE GIFT OF LOVE
THE GIVER, THE TAKER, THE MISERY
　　MAKER THE INJURED BIRD
THE MECHANICS OF LOVE
THE MYSTICISMS OF LIFE
THE PERPETUAL WINTER
ME
THE REAL ME
THE SANCTUARY
THE SWORD OF DAMOCLES
THE TORMENT OF TIME
THE TORMENTED TOAD
THE WEATHER OF THE HEART
UNANSWERABLE TEARS
UNREQUITED LOVE
WE ARE THE GREYS
WEATHER PATTERNS
WEB OF DECEIT
WEEP DEAR WILLOW LIKE ME
WHO OVERFILLED MY BUCKET?
WITHIN THE SEASONS OF MY
　　WETHERED SOUL

VILLANELLE

A THOUSAND-YARD STARE

As I sleepwalk with death, does my fellow man care?
I march down the street, with my bruised booted feet,
I'm a solitary guy, with a thousand-yard stare.

The calamities of war, no horrors compare,
I pass with head high, in pretence, no defeat,
As I sleepwalk with death, does my fellow man care?

I fought for my flag, was expectancy fair?
My eyes showing winter, with yours must not meet,
I'm a solitary guy, with a thousand-yard stare.

With torrents of untruths, always beware,
There are enemies within that stride down your street.
As I sleepwalk with death, does my fellow man care?

As a killing machine, I laid my heart bare,
I snuffed out my soul for this country so sweet,
I'm a solitary guy, with a thousand-yard stare.

Ambushed by my grief, no sanity's there?
With PTSD, I'm too exhausted to weep.
As I sleepwalk with death, does my fellow man care?
I'm a solitary guy, with a thousand-yard stare.

A BRIDGE TOO FAR

Crossing the city bridge, shafts of sleet moisten my wanton lips.
Below a shell of a home nurses the silences of her past.
To the loveless shown, she hugs her vandalised aching bones of rusty steel.
In time's torment she listens to the collision of chatter and the whoosh of wheels.

A snatch and grab of kaleidoscope graffiti streaks the underpass.
A broth of haematic strokes sprays its deep unanswered words to the gathering chuggers.
Sticks and crusty bleeding bricks scar the surly glazed gutters.
Nefarious needles, abandoned stubs toss their fire and brimstone calling cards.

A trainer with wordless tongue lay shipwrecked amongst the pebbles of cola cans.
Silvery pulled rings struggle to shine with their falseness of hope.
Soiled sodden sheets of past news huddle together like crumpled dreams.
Obscene lights from city shops hoodwink the juxtaposing jostlers.

Clutching with a savagery at the fullness of our empty shopping bags,
restless fingers search for plastic to feed the tugging tills, to acquire the heart's desires.
A penitent frowsy tramp prays for the green man to arrive.
With fist raised he mouths his solemn sermon to the lost flock.

An elderflower snakes its way out of a drab crumbling wall,
and unseen majestically displays its overripe tempting fruit.
In our brutal hunger for more, we grab without reason unwanted trinkets.
With our third blind eye, we stare blankly into the depths of our own ugliness.

We spendthrifts swarm like locusts, not for need, but for the hollow gratification of greed.
Leaving sorrow, to stalk us tomorrow, we grab at the now, and cross a bridge too far.

A CACOPHONY OF SOUND

I dip my toes into the frothing warm tide, gingerly checking the heat, and swing my other leg over the rim of the bath's rigid grin.

I plop my ample cellulite ass into the foam, still checking whether the undulating water is bearable. Yes, yes, I can stand the heat.

I slide the rest of my whale-like body below the surface, watching the frothy tide dip and rise around my curves, and give out an elongated puff and groan as all the screaming aches and pains of the day slowly dissipate into the curling mists swallowing up the bathroom.

I lie unable to move, like the lady of the lake, stiff as the silent dead, staring, staring corpse-like, at the walls of cold rigid tiles that coffin me. O the joy of doing nothing, absolutely nothing. I just want to BE.

I wallow in the softening of my grievances but cannot, however, switch off my brain. The thoughts of the day swirl around my aching head, worries once again march faster and faster into view with their heavy boots on, and armed with their artillery of weapons

I grab at my sodden sponge and attempt to swipe them away from my furrowed frown, but to no avail, they keep on yomping through the muddy tracks of my mind.

I will drown them, that's what I'll do, I'll drown them.

I slowly slide my blubber lower and lower into the comforting heat until my reddened face is all that is not submerged.

I feel tired, so tired. One, two, three. One, two, three. I will sink below the bobbing lavender and silk extracts of bubbles, never to breathe again, never to be burdened by overwhelming sorrows bought on by my umbrageous attitude. Never to be weighed down by the responsibilities of being daughter, wife, mother, friend, breadwinner. I want to be alone with me, just this rusting old carcass that's me.

I hold my breath as I muster up all the courage I have, to silently sink below the frothing waves like a submarine, never to be seen again.

I take one last suck at the damp air and hold my breath, ready for my demise.

From nowhere I hear a cacophony of sound blowing shoreward through the front door below. My mother calls out, 'Cooee.'

They are early, much too early. I hear her opening and shutting doors and calling out my name. Light footsteps tap their way up the wooden stairs.

My peace is shattered into fragments. The bathroom doorknob rattles as my five-year-old child screams, 'Mummy, Mummy, are you in there? How long are you going to be? I really, really need a poo!'

I sit bolt upright in the bath, and robotically pull the plug, letting death unspool itself down the drain.

'Alright, love, all right. Mummy won't be long.'

A smile tiptoes across my wet face as I realise my life has been saved by the need of a poo!

A DAY AT THE SEASIDE

A panting blue coach emblazoned with the words *Sky Tours* limps into a parking spot at Weston-super-Mare front. A balding middle-aged man pops out of the driver's door like a cork from a bottle and hops around to the main door of the coach, which he slams open. Fred, a short wiry man, is the first to alight and skips onto the pavement to demonstrate the little vitality he still has left. He fluffs up his feathers and flashes a chilling sideways glance at the driver as he snatches the door handle from his grasp.

A woman's voice booms from the coach, 'Can someone help Marge off the coach? I've got her stick. Come on, Fred, you can help her but be careful… careful now.'

Marge groans as she alights. 'Phoof! Thank goodness we are off that damn coach. I think I have a square ass.'

'Are you alright, Marge?' asks Alma, following on behind, waving Marge's stick.

Her voice is suddenly drowned by the loud cries of seagulls and the clatter of Zimmers and a wheelchair being unloaded by the driver onto the pavement, proving his point.

'Stop fussing,' snaps Marge. 'Anyone would think I was a piece of Dresden china. Gosh, it's blowing a gale here, and look at those damn clouds. We couldn't have picked a worse—'

'Well, I feel excited,' bubbles Alma. 'We should have

bought our buckets and spades. Look, Marge, look. There is the sea.'

Marge gazes out into the horizon with her crooked arthritic hand cocked over a deep frown that had found its way onto her brow and was refusing to disappear. 'Where? It's such a long way out. I would need to borrow Mabel's mobility scooter if I wanted to get to it, which, as it happens, I don't. Anyway, I would probably sink up to my neck in mud before I got there. Look at the state of that water. It looks horrible, horrible, just like gravy.'

'Stop making that face, Marge,' snaps Alma. 'If this wind changes direction, you'll stay like that.'

'Shut up, Alma,' Marge snaps back.

'There are the donkeys over there. Oh, look at them, Marge. Aren't they lovely? Do you think at my age I could have a ride on them? Wouldn't that be smashing?'

'Oh, for goodness' sake, Alma. Anyway, you're too fat to get on one of those. They'll sink to their knees, poor buggers, with your weight on them.'

Alma, who has always seen the world with a light in her eyes, pauses for a second before replying. 'Well, I'm going over there to ask that nice man if I can have a go. My parents never had much money when I was little. I've never been on a donkey. Come to think of it, I never had a real holiday either.'

Marge pulls up the faded collar of her grey quilted jacket, trying to block out the breeze nibbling at her neck. 'Come on, Alma, don't be so stupid. Let's follow the rest and sit in the café near the pier and have a nice cup of tea.'

'Tea, tea, tea,' shouts Alma. 'That's the highlight of our

lives at our age. Just to sit and drink damn tea. And as for poor old Fred, he will be in and out of the toilets with his bladder just like one of those Weston donkeys.'

'Grow up, Alma, grow up,' retorts Marge.

'I hate being old. I want to feel young again before it's too late. You go with the rest. I'm having a ride on the donkeys and then I'm going to have the biggest candy floss I can find.' Alma's voice is eaten up once again by the cacophony of seagull cries and the chattering of false teeth. Suddenly, her voice finds itself again and fills the air with 'The Sun Has Got His Hat On, Hip-hip-hip Hooray'.

Marge, tutting, leans on her stick and disassociates herself from her friend. She slowly hobbles to the café where Fred, bent double, is doing a quick scan of the rain-soaked menu board over his steamed-up bifocals.

'Well, girls,' he announces proudly, straightening himself up and cracking his knuckles, 'the price of the tea is reasonable and we could even push the boat out and have a cream scone each.' Fred enjoys being the cock of the north with all his brood of hens around him. He now, at last, has pride of place in life, what with him being the last man standing.

The huddle of whittering women slowly shuffle to the café, their permed grey heads bobbing in the breeze.

'Ah, here's a nice table. We'll just move all the chairs together,' calls Marge, giving orders but not making any attempt to help – after all, she has a stick. Everyone plays the usual game of musical chairs, all checking where they will sit. Are they in draughts? Can they get in and out to the toilets OK? Is there somewhere for their coats and walking aids? Round and round the tables they shuffle, one behind the other. 'Gosh, I don't believe it. There's a chink in the clouds; the sun's finally trying to show its face,' calls out Marge. 'Let's hope it doesn't shine too much in our eyes. It's bad enough with my cataracts or we'll all have to move and sit somewhere else. I can't stand the sun in my face. Are you all happy where you are?'

Grunts of 'Yes, yes' are followed by the scraping and banging of chairs against the tables and the dragging noise of metal across the wooden floor. One chair has to be moved to make room for Elsie's wheelchair. A couple of Zimmer frames are piled into the corner. Puffs, moans and groans follow as aged polyester plump bums are firmly parked on the peeling wooden chairs. They all check each other is alright.

'It's not too cold for you by the door, is it, Fred?' Marge asks indifferently, thanking the Lord she is not sitting where he is.

'Well, it is a bit, but I will have to grin and bear it, but thanks for asking, Marge. Hang on a minute, we're one short. Where's Alma?' asks Fred.

'Oh, I don't know. I think she's wandered off, you know what she is like when she has one of her paddies,' snaps Marge.

Fred peers vacantly out of the window of the café until something catches his attention out of the corner of his eye. 'Who's that?' he enquires.

'Where?' asks Marge.

'Over there,' points Fred with his bent finger. 'Over there with a kiss-me-quick hat on, sat on a donkey.'

'Oh my God, it's Alma,' cries Marge. 'What's she doing making a spectacle of herself like that?'

'Leave her alone, Marge, for goodness' sake,' begs Fred. 'The lassie's enjoying herself for once. Anyway, she needs to now.'

'What do you mean by *now*?'

'Didn't she tell you?' replies Fred, fidgeting on his chair and feeling a little uncomfortable.

'Tell me what?'

'I know I've let the cat out of the bag, but she was diagnosed with terminal cancer last week. She wouldn't tell me where, but I think it must be somewhere secret. Maybe something to do with women's bits and bobs. She obviously didn't want to tell you and worry you, what with you being her best friend,' says Fred, lowering his voice and cracking his knuckles again.

A tangible silence fills the air, followed by a scuffing of a chair as Marge springs to life.

'Where are you going, Marge?' enquires Fred.

'With or without my bloody stick, I'm going to have a ride on a donkey with my best friend.'

A DUSTING OF DEATH

Pondering on life's mockery with black beaded eyes,
He lay stuck like a placenta to the clammy walls of the highway's womb.
His aquiline beak mouths silently in the finality of his future.
The full stop blots the unfinished sentence.

Pinions scratch an epitaph upon the slippery slate.
Voracious steeds scream with a whoosh, whoosh, whoosh,
And whip up the despondency of feathers that cannot fly.
Upturned claws unpick the universal paradigm of nature.

Flawed diamond motes crown his scrawny head.
Haematic snowflakes fall softly from his grimacing grin,
As he exudes his unheard asinine words to the congregation of shadows,
Gathering en masse in the solemn grievances of the night.

Murdering echoes scour the bloodstained mantle of the motorway,
Whilst earth's rusty urn stands awaiting, for the minion with a dusting of death.

HAIKU

A HOST OF SPARROWS

A host of sparrows.
What destruction did you bring,
Decimating crops?

A LEAF IN THE CHAPTER OF WAR

Upon the cold uncaring brow of winter,
When time with no meaning has silently splintered.
A shy, solitary, ragged dressed leaf,
Struggles amongst the gunshots of disbelief.

Down, down lady dances to death's dying beat,
As guns tap their feet, whilst souls left to weep.
Drawn to the gates of hell, void of all hope,
In the far side of despair lonely hands grope.

Spiralling, spinning, to greet gaunt ghosts of man,
Soaked in poppy-red blood in faraway lands.
With a sad soul in the madness, she silently rests,
By the soiled sullied figure gasping for breath.

Trembling as one the leaf light as a feather,
Caresses his cheek as thy both die together.

A PEACEFUL SATISFACTION

A distant fanfare calls to my inner self and stirs my pensive soul.
A rose flame of inspiration flashes, from which illuminated I write.
The dawn breaks across the mantle of my unvarnished words,
vanishing the greyness snagged amongst the branches of my thoughts.

From the broth of emotions and a flickering of insight, creation ignites.
My pockets fill with dry words which I must wax to bring out the best of me.
The briefness of the day casts its strange light, shaping my imagination.
Iambic pentameters soothe the chaos of the surrendering hours.

In the creeping of the eventide, I peacefully pen beneath the pearl moon.
Snatches of words beat their luminous wings and travel towards the light,
Sparking my misty mind with lines that can be felt.
Completion of verse, I bask in the bright side of my blank wall.

In my ebullience I am truly blessed by the unfounded optimism,
of another creation, which keeps up a cheerfulness in my mind.

A SNOWY CHRISTMAS

Falling upon the frozen mantle of the earth,
Are the softest whispers spoken with icy breaths.
Fluttering feather-like on winter's chilled grave,
A phantasmal transformation is taking place,
As innocent children peacefully sleep.

Snowflakes spread a virginal sheet,
A dusting, of the purest, celestial white,
Where Santa's footprints will stealthily creep.
Light, as a clear conscience, in the night,
A quietus frost sparkles, crowning the silence with its jewels.

Whilst the snow spreads its tapestry of crystal kisses,
Church carols begin riding the backs of echoes,
And as the church bells chime, in unison, their blessings,
We are re-assured of good times to come,
Filled with joy and redemption.

Smothering the bare bones of boughs,
In a comforting winter fleece,
Snowflakes flitter, in the rejoicing,
Of their ebullient freedom, from the empyrean,
And tenderly trace twigs, with their intricate designs.

Nature's healing hands balm the night sky,
With exuberant dust, which dances in the gentle breeze,
and powders and puffs our hoary headed homes.
Flakes frolic frenetically, in expectation,
Of our Christmas wishes.

Floating down from the Heavens,
The snow rejoices in the purity it bestows.
A rising phantom of hope from the gelid skies,
Fills with joy, the treachery of the season,
And seeks solace, within its own serene space.

As a luminescent star shines its leading light,
Snowflakes soothe my raddled thoughts,
Assisting me to recall,
At this very special time of giving,
The true meaning of Christmas.

My mind is filled with wonder,
At the virginal scene surrounding me.
I am in awe, at the radiancy of glory, I behold,
Which holds my heart hostage,
And purges my restless spirit.

Within the constituency of my thoughts,
As the silence, again,
Is suddenly splintered,
By the distant sound of sleigh bells,
My rocky path is rendered lighter.

And as I rest my pen in contemplation,
On this mystical, magical, snowy night.
I wish you a very Merry Christmas filled with love.

HAIKU

A TAPPING

*Who is that tapping,
Tapping at my door at night,
With grim winter nails?*

PANTOUM

A WANDERING ROAD

Outside a gold dipped sun attempts to smile between the clusters of cloud scudding its face.
I hesitate to open myself to a world of madness to let the future in, fearing what I may see.
A wandering road beckons, and bestows a faint trail of hope upon my apathy.
Losing direction, this seasoned traveller pauses by a river of thoughts, pursuing her identity.

I hesitate to open myself to a world of madness to let the future in, fearing what I may see.
I realise with a fake smile I will soon have to walk another lonely path that invites my tread.
Losing direction, this seasoned traveller pauses by a river of thoughts, pursuing her identity.
Memories like autumn leaves blow across my path, seeking refuge in their own dark space.

I realise with a fake smile I will soon have to walk another lonely path that invites my tread.
Curses and consequences knock on my door, binding me to the empty solace of my room.

*Memories like autumn leaves blow across my path,
　seeking refuge in their own dark space.
With a broth of doubts, I trek through my solitary griefs
　that lead nowhere and are endless.*

*Curses and consequences knock on my door, binding me
　to the empty solace of my room.
Outside a gold dipped sun attempts to smile between the
　clusters of cloud scudding its face.
With a broth of doubts, I trek through my solitary griefs
　that lead nowhere and are endless.
A wandering road beckons and bestows a faint trail of
　hope upon my apathy.*

PANTOUM

A WINTER'S STORY

In the pitiless attrition, the fluttering of snow silently drifts.
Angels hover, and softly spread their pristine white wings.
I will write upon the descent of death with the lines of love and life,
In the bleak tenebrous days of winter, covered with its frost of woes.

Angels hover, and softly spread their pristine white wings.
Blanketing my lonely footprints, stamped amongst the ruins of winter.
In the bleak tenebrous days of winter, covered with its frost of woes.
Befuddled cobwebs trail from dead limbs and defiant blood-red berries.

Blanketing my lonely footprints, stamped amongst the ruins of winter,
The mantle of the earth lies still and buried within its frozen tomb.

Befuddled cobwebs trail from dead limbs and defiant blood-red berries.
The tyranny of frost is apparent as the blank pages of the fields lie wordless.

The mantle of the earth lies still and buried within its frozen tomb.
In the pitiless attrition the fluttering of snow silently drifts.
The tyranny of frost is apparent as the blank pages of the fields lie wordless.
I will write upon the descent of death with the lines of love and life.

ABORTION

Faded dreams, hopes bright declined,

Cherished memories will never be mine.

Intense the pain but not in limb,

My existence was gouged from deep within.

Sedative for narcotic state,

My being I had to exuviate.

Nature, why so cruel and kind?

If one life to take, leave my baby behind.

PANTOUM

ABSENT FRIENDS

We remain in contemplation, beneath the boughs of our silent seclusion.
Trapped within a quietus meditation, we unearth tender memories.
We will, therefore, always remember with fondness, our absent friends,
As time perpetually plucks its tune upon the strings of our hearts.

Trapped within a quietus meditation, we unearth tender memories.
Within our darkest moments of loss, may we always see the light.
As time perpetually plucks its tune upon the strings of our hearts,
Old alliances brighten like stars, the deficiencies of our world.

Within our darkest moments of loss, may we always see the light.
May we, eternally be united, by the handshake of camaraderie.
Old alliances brighten like stars, the deficiencies of our world.
Leaving a legacy of friendship behind, makes the world a happier place.

May we, eternally be united, by the handshake of camaraderie.
We remain in contemplation, beneath the boughs of our silent seclusion,
Leaving a legacy of friendship behind, makes the world a happier place.
We will, therefore, always remember with fondness, our absent friends.

ADDICTION

In the depths of my nicotine-stained room,
Only he and I exist,
Breathlessly speaking,
With glorious smoking tongues.
My phoenix rises from the ashes,
And scrawls big Cs upon my ceiling.
I pay no heed to the warning,
Tattooed with tar on my walls,
"Smoking Kills".
His odorous breath next to mine,
Drowns my mind, with cravings.
Wispy fingers fondle my clothes,
Filling my pockets with stale perfume.
Without a flicker of remorse,
He threatens to stub out my future.
My resistance fades,
Tangled sinews ignite,
And in my weakness,
I reach out for his tempting lips,
Yearning for the kiss of death.

AGED MOLE

Perplexed in a coal-black room of loneliness,
turning pale with indifference, shuffling.
A squeezing of my wheezing lungs,
lost consonants, vowels, muddled in the muffling.
Approaching, with apprehension, tangled roots,
of Heaven, or is it Hell?
I fought from my hills with loud opinions,
now coffined in my defence I dwell.
A prisoner hopelessly wandering,
through darkened tunnels of accelerated time.
Stonkered, I spade in my blindness,
around twisted truths in a wavering line.

ALONG THE BRUTAL SHORES OF MY WORLD

The shadowy ghosts of my former self stretch out from my feet,
Like tides of flat floundering dabs, along the cold solitary beach.
The grainy air swallows up the inaudible cursing of my misery.
The sap of suffering corkscrews me into the curvaceous dunes.
My grunts and groans bubble and foam in the rip-rap of hurt,
Surfing my ulcered mouth like a salient sweet.
Memoires stain my mind with their oil polluting piercing ink.
Re-enactments of events are shaped in the currents of my spiralling drop.
Ocean-masters race up my spine, pricking the corners of my consciousness.
Swirling and shunted in the tide's brainstorm of pain,
Like the driftwood's face pushed into the sand,
I spit out the grains of sadness and crawl towards the sea.
The battle of breathing in the tempest becomes a chore.
No rescuing ethereal hand in the stinging shards of rain.
My eyes hurt seeing the vacancy the blackened flow of the sea.
I rise and fall like the determined waves screaming out to the breaking of the day,
As I smash myself to pieces along the brittle shores of my drowning world.

AMID THE WINTER SNOW

The canker of the crude earth,
Lies sugary and sweetened,
By the spreading of the angels',
Pristine white wings.

In the face of the charismatic foe,
Red-bloodied berries burst forth,
In strong defiance,
From ice-coated spicule leaves.

In the bleak tenebrous winter,
Covered with a frost of woes,
Befuddled cobweb tendons trail,
From naked limb to brittle leaf.

We snare and store the ghostly vision,
Deep within our mind's dusty corners.
An architecture of quivering warps and wefts,
Displayed in snow's snuffling, soft-spoken breath.

Untamed chaste snow-capped hills,
Stab mercilessly at the bloated leaded sky,
Ready to burst the buttress of dreamlike,
Pink and purple bubble balloons.
Armed with resentment,
The ravaging raw breeze hunts in the forests,
Where unrelentless hunger stalks,
And mercilessly bites at each frozen heart.

In the pitiless attrition,
The fluttering of shedding skin faintly falls.
The tyranny of frost is apparent,
As the calcifying pages of fields lie dormant.

Too fearful to move,
Smothered beneath their virginal blanket,
The mantle of the earth lies still,
Buried within its frozen tomb.

Touched by the treacherous cold hand,
Of a nefarious sorcerer,
I gaze upon death's descent,
Which precedes spring's life.

Mirrored in pond's glass,
Lies nature's ambushed reflection,
Displaying in its grim harshness,
A certain tortured grief.

Wrapped in the stinging silence,
And solitude of subservient surroundings,
And the acceptance of what will be,
I find my quietude and unspool my heart.

Entombed in the ruins of frost,
Amongst my lonely footprints,
A chaste snowdrop waves her frills of truce,
Displaying hope in the peace of the day.

SESTINA

AN UNKINDNESS OF RAVENS

Black acrobats like blindness fall,
tumbling, fumbling, cursing call,
and watch with the eye at the back of their head,
and gather by the murdered dead.
With ruinous hearts the stonewallers
gorge on victim's fleshy bones.

My addict stamps on dense skull bone,
and wanton sees my spirits fall.
With lifeless eyes and stony
stare, prruk my carrion calls.
You peck, peck, peck a soul that's dead,
and pack with wars my withered head.

Cloaked wizards with charred spikey heads,
cast their spells on scavenged bones.
With Bowie-knife beaks they hunt the dead,
and circling cleave their fall.
Hell's undertakers croak their calls,
of discourse over earth's hearthstones.

With roving eyes that chill the stone,
the miners shake their sooty heads.
Frosty owls with faithful calls,

fluff and puff their bone-
pale breasts, whilst the moon's smile falls
away they hoot to the long sleep of the dead.

A bearded darkling drops its cloak upon the living dead,
wrapping up sad faces shattered by life's stone.
Dance my harbinger of doom, feast on my freefall,
I try to flee but find your tracks are thorns within my head.
I scuttle like a mouse to shield my snow bough bones,
from east to west I search for peace before my raven calls.

The unkindness of the ravens, hear their tuneless calls,
in the spilling of the seconds before the day lies dead.
The wind whips up a long-felt rage rattling like a bone,
and wipes away the tears I cry that cannot crack my stone.
Caustic are your comments sealed inwards in my head.
You pleasure in my pain so you will not catch my fall.

I will just be, not fall, when my sinful raven calls.
The full moon in my head casts no shadows on the dead.
I am not your stepping stone. Fly free, my spirit, from the
   bone.

AN UNWANTED VISITOR

The night cold and fresh as a newly dug grave drops like a stone upon the dank earth. A rogue raincloud stalks the darkness and whips the stagnant dull mirror in the bottom acre. It cries for the wandering soul who already has a place booked at the gates of Hell.

An old man stung by sorrow coughs and gobs his phlegm onto the glowing fire. It hisses and spits back at the huddled frame. He slowly picks up the iron poker and prods it menacingly with his clawed hand in retaliation of its defiance, bringing the dying flames back to life with a crackle and splutter.

Fred stares blindly into the burning embers. Tormented shadows dance across the furrows of his brow and his leathered face splintered by life. His worn flat cap, greasy with age, squats on his head like a squashed toad trying to keep his thoughts from wandering. A candle curls its vapours up into a corner of his room and drips its bronze blood over a wooden table in its cremation. Fred is very thrifty. Who needs light bulbs? The moon appears once more and fires its arrows through the gaping holes in the yellowing net curtains, once hung with love, and stabs at the cracks of the cell with its fine shavings of bone. Cold tears shine in the corners of Fred's cloudy eyes, which are as dead as his grief, and his stiffened ears remain cocked, listening like the wild beasts in the fields for the slightest sound of danger in the deafening silence.

Fred sold his land to the developer who had been chasing him for many years. The fight has gone out of him and all that is left is the flight. All he wants now is to be left alone. Smoke from the candle acids his eyes. He wipes them gently with a filthy stained handkerchief found in his pocket, and coughs once again through brittle cracked lips to relieve his tension. He clears his throat before wiping the dribble oozing from the corners of his mouth.

The shrunken farmer, living his half death, remains huddled in his threadbare chair. Life had not materialised as he had hoped for. Dreams had faded and dropped away into a chasm of resentment. There were no sons or even daughters to work the land; him and his wife were not blessed. Maybe that was her problem. She was barren as the harsh top acres. He once again tries to unpick the threads of the past and reweave them into fiction, to justify all the events that had happened. A moth flutters around the candle's flame and, touching its fate, singes its delicate glass wings.

Fred recalls the pond in the centre of his land where ducks swam, and frogs croaked in their calling site in the ever-changing face of nature. Reeds like twisted lanes held a multitude of life. It had eventually lost its fight for survival and died, and became an ugly scar, holding on to the stagnancy of its secret. The developers want to keep the pond to make a feature of it on the estate, after they have removed all the silt and poison from its grasp. *What a feature*, thinks Fred. The old home groans with pain and Fred shivers slightly as the room chills. Armed with the dead weight of the past, he pokes the fire again, demanding its warmth, knowing all the while it is him that is burnt out, not the fire.

Suddenly he hears it, and stiffens like a stook. Yes, there it is again – a scratching. The wooden boards outside the butter-stone cottage creak, snapping their teeth at the night. 'Who's there?' he growls, hoping for a reply, but none comes. He once again clears his throat. The moon disappears behind its buttress of cloud, adding to the atmosphere of panic. A fox's cry fills the lower Cotswold meadow like a child in pain, making the old farmer jump.

Fred, haunted by the worst of himself, curls back into the comfort of his chair, as he draws a sour breath. *I wonder if they will dredge the pond and restore it to its former glory soon?* he ponders. The digger had positioned itself beside the once crystal-clear waters, mocking Fred with its harsh hostile wide grin, and bearing its metal teeth. Days it has silently stood, devouring time. Fred did not want to go down to the pond to see what was happening; he could see enough from his window.

Suddenly the scratching begins again. Night after night the visitor comes to his door, ever since he signed the land over to the developers three months ago. A scratching like chalk scraped down a blackboard, long and slow. 'Go away, go away, whoever you are,' rasps Fred frozen in fright, and asthmatically coughs. 'What do you want of me?' he calls, again with words of desperation drying in his mouth. Nails drag down the door, scraping, scraping away at the peeling paint. Fred jumps up, forgetting his arthritis. The hairs on his neck stand to attention as he shivers. He swings around and grabs the iron poker and brandishes it like a sword. 'Come on then, you bugger, come on.' He hears a whisper – or was it the wind? His hearing is not as sharp as it used to be. Shapes of darkness uncoil and dance across his walls and crawl across his ceiling, mocking his fear.

He picks out the murmuring words – yes, he can hear them. 'Fred, Fred,' she calls. He has that voice imprinted on his mind. The cruel necessity of constant nagging had filled his past until he could no longer stand it in his life, and now once again that same voice has come back to haunt him. 'Fred, Fred,' she cries again. 'Shut up, shut up. Leave me alone,' Fred shouts, calling out to the nothingness in the thick smog of his smoky room.

He knew in his heart what is coming next. The latch suddenly clicks and rises, trying to crack the door alive, but the bolt holds firm. He stares down to the chipped quarry tiled floor where the old stable door locks out the evils of the night. There, there it was again, sliding under the door. Slowly and menacingly, the ghostly dark fingers slither towards him. The oily slick, black as blindness itself, slowly grows larger and feels its way, crawling, crawling towards Fred. The silted dark blood soaks into Fred's slippers. 'Enid, Enid, leave me alone. What do you want of me?' A cackle fills the air and echoes around his icy space. Fred stands alone in his room where love had lost its way many years ago. He cannot open the door, for he knows he will be staring into the shrunken eyes of death. Terror takes its hold; his heavy heartbeat quickens until it beats outside of itself. Louder and louder it thumps. He draws one last painful breath and crumples onto the floor, clutching at his chest as the walls busied by damp close in and swallow him up. A shadow floats between him and the shining light of the moon, and touches his ploughed forehead with its icy immortal hands.

The funeral is a sombre occasion, with very few mourners attending, held between the local church's crumbling grey walls. The manager of Hill Rise Homes turns up to show a fleeting respect.

A few curled-up ham and cheese sandwiches are laid on after the service at 'The Brown Bear'. Mr Edwards' mobile rings as he stands upright in the corner of the pub, clutching an Old Ric. He juggles with his beer and mobile phone. 'Hill Rise Homes, Mr Edwards speaking… O, hi George. What… what are you saying? Repeat it again. In the pond, you found what? For God's sake, George! Ring the police, quick, quick!'

AS THE STARS BLOW OUT OF THE SKY

Split like a dropped melon, the cycle helmet bounces down the road and comes to rest in a damp clump of grass frilling the edge of the gravel. All lies still in the empty space of the darkness except for the tick, ticking of a wheel next to broken branches, spinning round and round, which tries to keep pace with the torrent of time. It finally gives up the ghost and slowly grinds to a halt in the framework of silence.

A full moon shines out from the pocket of the dark night, casting itself upon the shadow of an injured man.

Ken can feel sharp needles of pain piercing his body, forcing him to drift in and out of the comfort of his dreams, pushing him shoreward towards the nightmares of a harsh reality.

He forces his heavy eyelids open and stares into the blindness of the night through a warm trickle of blood, which meanders down his face from his forehead. His arms are spreadeagled. Through a frown of concentration, he looks upwards to the unmasked moon and into the star-spangled night and tries to understand what has just happened to him. Ken remains perfectly still and, realising he has fallen off his bike, tries not to cause more damage to himself. Has he broken his neck? It is a terror he does not want to visit, so he quickly tries to quieten his mind. A piercing pain returns to greet him. He tries to breathe but can only manage short shallow breaths as his lungs will not inflate properly. Ken lays panting like a dog anticipating instructions from its owner.

Is he alone? He realises to his horror that there is a leg next to his body, lying in the opposite direction. It cannot be his, surely. He releases the cold stones trapped between his grubby fingers and slowly raises his left hand across his body to feel the leg. A violent torrent of panic takes hold with the realisation that the shattered leg is, in fact, his own.

I must not move, he instructs himself, *in case I do more damage. Have I broken my neck as well?* He lies as still and as silent as the dead, staring, staring up into the loneliness of the night sky with a fear fettered to his eyes. A tear drops from Ken's cheek into a cloudy puddle by his face. Ken lifts once more his bleeding hand and reaches for the mobile in his pocket and dials for an ambulance. For a split second in time, he has forgotten where he is and then, through the fog of forgetfulness, the past becomes clear. He should never have gone to the Rose and Crown. He stayed much longer than anticipated. Ken knew, in his heart, that this accident is nothing but retribution, but he is not yet ready to step into the darkness of that thought.

Ken taps his mobile with urgency and tells the emergency services roughly where he is, but their reply is not comforting. They will send an ambulance when one is available, but they are overstretched at present. *Available? Available?!* he queries, as he wipes a trickle of blood in the cuff of his brown waterproof jacket. Through the pain of understanding his position and the plodding of reasoning in his aching brain, he tries to retain a shallow politeness and thanks them.

Ken helplessly drops his mobile onto the cold unforgiving stones that lie spotted and dotted among putrefied puddles in the meandering lane. The bumpy, lumpy lane that skirts the fertile fields.

Ken's mind goes back to the meeting he attended in the room at the back of the pub. Many of the local residents turned up – even the local farmer arrived in his tractor after working on his land. The air in the meeting was dry and acrid, which left the public with a desperate thirst for what was right, and although Ken knew what was right, he kept running back to hide behind his false identity.

The local farmer, who had appeared from nowhere, took him on like a rutting stag. He had a thunderous untamed voice and yelled out all of his complaints through an excess of spittle, which showered all and sundry in his line of fire. His boiling face peeked out through his filthy flat cap as he attempted to make his point with aggressive gestures. He flayed his arms like an injured bird trying to fly. He told the crowd that the lanes around the village had become inaccessible and two horse-riders from the local stables had injured themselves when their horses had fallen, all due to the council's lack of funds.

Ken was the only councillor who had attended the meeting and so he'd had to take on the battle alone. He'd been appointed to chair the meeting and, being the newest councillor, needed to prove his worth. He'd tried to calm the local crowd as he wrestled with his slippery words, but the villagers were like hounds baying for blood and he was the fox. Ken listened with deaf ears to all of their complaints, then rose up and spoke like a calm, calculating machine, spilling out objectives. He knew he must not let the crowd rile him or it would demonstrate an absence of self-control and also question his public education. The villagers, however, knew, deep down inside, that no matter what they said, Ken would be the arbiter of their fate.

The villagers had fought and fought for the council to release money for their cause, but their voices fell on deaf ears. There was only a certain amount of money available in the council's coffers as there had been large cuts to the money allocated to them.

The pain of Ken's injuries arrives again, knocking loudly at his door, banging, banging once again to be let in. *Where is the ambulance?* Ken begins shivering uncontrollably in the after-silence of his accident. A coldness flows through his veins but he knows he must not succumb to the blessings of sleep. His breathing becomes more laboured and, with every breath, he feels the hands of death squeezing his throat.

His pallid skin is covered with a damp grey mist and shines luminously beneath the full moon. A satanic bat with leathered wings flitters by and a knowing owl hoots in the distance as Ken lies weeping in the wilderness. *Alas*, he consoles himself, *there is still life out there.*

Ken's mind somersaults back to the council meeting held at the Rose and Crown. Did he believe in what he was saying to the villagers? Not really. He was just lost in the superfluity of his barren words.

He knows they are right, but what could he do? The lanes and roads in and around the village had become very dangerous due to the many deep potholes appearing from nowhere, and the villagers knew there could be more people on bikes or horses who would be seriously injured because of them. There was also the damage to the cars hitting the potholes. Repairs could be very costly. Ken knew when he entered the meeting that he could only console them and that they had lost the battle before it had begun.

Ken gently sighs once more into the darkness, cloaking him with its extended wings, and – surprisingly, being atheist – calls out to God, alas with hollow words, of which he uses frequently.

Suddenly, he hears a rumbling in the distance, like thunder. Long lights appear from afar and spread out their fingers, groping at the chaos spread out in the middle of the lane. The weather turns itself around and a breeze picks up, carrying the echoes of the rattling noise, which get louder and louder.

A fear grabs hold of Ken by the throat as he realises it is the sound of a tractor and it is not slowing down but getting faster and faster.

He closes his eyes for one last time as the stars blow out of the sky.

BEIGE JACKETS

Beige jackets. Beige jackets everywhere. Essential clothing as you rapidly decline into old age. My father cherished one; so worn, so shabby it could have walked away on its own. Polyester, it has to be polyester. Void of any style, resting just below the waist. Straight up, straight down, a vision of lollipop sticks with silver crowns.

The grey brigade continually struggle up and down high streets in their compulsory uniforms. Sometimes somebody breaks rank and wears an identical jacket but silver-grey. Sticks, Zimmer frames, disability scooters all kitted out the same, with beige jacketed frail companions shuffling around in the mimicry of life. Camouflaged within the nondescript background of life, the dying melt away, never to be remembered.

I am an old-aged pensioner but give me scarlet jeans and crippling sparkly shoes – in any bright colour, with highest heels and styles so chic – that clitter-clatter down the street.

People may laugh at my rainbow colours and people may stare. Colour is the vibrancy of life, why would I care?

When life is through and I cannot hack it, please don't leave me at the heavenly gates swaddled in a beige jacket.

BELLY DANCING IN BIRKENHEAD

Enid rolls the pea-sized Blu-tack around her sweaty palms until it resembles freshly chewed gum and pops it into her umbilicus followed by a plastic ruby.

'There,' she mutters to herself. 'That should hold it.'

Enid glances across the stage at the chattering ladies all fiddling and fussing with their plus-size fiery silks (polyester), which sparkle and shine like freshly stoked fires illuminating the dimly lit Methodist Hall.

Fiona, the instructor, focuses her eyes on her flock of over sixties, brimming with enthusiasm and not much else. Cheap rainbow-coloured costume jewellery snatches and grabs at the odd ray of light, sending a kaleidoscope of colour dancing and leaping across the pale green washed-out walls of the hall. A hopelessness takes hold of Fiona as she spots the pale sagging skin and hypodermis pushing its way out of coin-covered hip belts and gypsy skirts. Some wear beaded bandanas, holding their tight grey perms in place.

'Now, girls,' Fiona shrills. 'Remember: horizontal, vertical, horizontal, vertical. Right, left, right, left. Remember to undulate to the beat.'

Fiona marches down the hall to fling open the brown peeling doors of the John Wesley Methodist Hall to let the first few reluctant family members in. Fred has finished fiddling with the lighting and, at last, has the music under control.

When the fuggy hall finally fills, Fiona takes a deep breath and introduces herself to the fidgeting audience. She tells them with pride that the evening is a charity event to raise money for the Donkey Forever Care Home in Hurghada, Egypt. She continues to tell them this is appropriate as belly dancing originated in Egypt and it is not because her group look like a bunch of donkeys!

'The dancing you are about to see is very expressive, consisting of complex movements of the torso, so give a big hand to our brave ladies.'

There is a loud encore and the pulsating music begins. The curtains open and, one by one, the belly dancers appear, shimmying and shaking their bellies. The coins around their swivelling hips swing and bounce to the music of the night. One of Flora's coins escapes from under its canopy of flab and pings on the stage floor. The wobbling flab beneath the belly dancers' arms swing to the rhythm like pale sails billowing in the breeze, and their painful arthritic fingers wriggle and point into the nothingness, trying to tell a story all of their own.

Faster and faster they gyrate, taking themselves back to their youthfulness and distant dreams of unfulfilled travels – most going no further than the sands of Blackpool. But they are here, here on the stage, giving it all they have, like lumps of Turkish Delight full of eastern promise.

Suddenly, without warning, Rose – who has a vast abundance of flesh on show – catches her foot in her billowing green pantaloons and crashes like a charging rhino into the next in line, sending all of them in a domino effect, crashing onto the stage. The blazing colours lay splattered, like dollops of acrylic paint on an artist's palette.

A gasp rises from the hall as people sit motionless in their seats. Fred stops the music as Fiona rushes to their aid.

Rose rises with only one gold slipper on, exposing her throbbing red bunion on her left foot. There is a gaping hole in her green silk pantaloons where she caught her foot. Flora's hip belt with threads dangling has slipped to her knees. Six coins have taken flight. Marge hastily pulls up her purple polyester pantaloons, hoping nobody has seen her beige full-length Sloggi briefs covering her ample backside.

Enid rises slowly with her gypsy skirt skew-whiff. Her bandana, having slipped, makes her look like a pirate with one short-sighted eye covered. She desperately tries to compose herself and coughs nervously.

Fiona rushes forward, clocking the *Gazette* reporter lingering near the stage with camera in hand and wearing a shady smile. He gives her a menacing wink.

The ladies assemble themselves and, under Fiona's instructions, complete their shortened sequence with a bow. They attempt to look as graceful as they can, but suddenly Enid spots a ruby glistening on the stage. She glances down and spots a lump of blue tack wriggling its head out of her belly button, and blushes inwardly.

In the John Wesley Methodist Hall on a dull October evening, in a mishmash of colour and chaos, east meets west.

BIRD BROOCH

Released from captivity,
From a Cirencester cage.
A prisoner bird acquires,
Its belief in its own immortality.

The once-lost Amphitheatre bird,
Ruffles its enamelled crimson wings,
In preparation to take flight and flee,
Into Heaven's brocaded tapestry.

Zoomorphic brooch,
In Roman times,
Did you clasp a heavy heart,
Weighted down with doubts?

Were you a precious gift,
Given with love,
Then cast idly aside,
Like a rose that has wilted and died?

Beneath the flower-filled fields you lay,
Until history triumphed over time.
And from the tomb of the earth,
We rejoiced in your rebirth.

When the world in its innocence sleeps,
And dark agents stealthily creep,
Shine, dear bird, like our morning light,
Amongst the arrival of the witching night.

With the beating of your wings,
O wondrous work of art.
Fly in freedom, fly,
Amongst the star-strewn sky.

In the museum's conspiracy of silence,
Amongst the antiquities which escaped time.
The sweetest note can be heard,
From the awakening beauteous bird.

HAIKU

BLEEDING HEART

I tried to be cold,
And unfeeling and frozen.
But my heart bled through.

BLINDED BY NORMALITY

Tracery scratches soiled
By the sinking of the day,
Dissipate in the Occident,
Where the sunset scolds the eye.
The luminescent moon
Rises upon us humans,
Who wander aimlessly,
And, maybe, should not exist.
What wretched creatures,
We have become,
Jostling on this sacred earth,
For position.
What is our purpose?
Can I play the game,
And be like everyone else?
Can I really be myself,
Without fear of ridicule?
Can I connect to other beings,
With my own frequency?
Can we all be moved,
To a higher vibration?
Can we all be connected,
By an umbilical cord,
A spiderweb of light energies,

And become one,
On this overcrowded earth?
What remains of us
Fustian foolish mortals,
Prickling with prejudices?
Compliantly we cower,
Within our corruptive societies,
Which have their knees on our necks,
Seeking the shallowness of acceptance,
But blinded by normality.

BOB

I first saw Bob at the fairground that was being held on the local common across the road from my house.

That was ten years ago, when I was an excitable, naïve eighteen-year-old.

Pushing through the crowds, I went across to where he was, drawn by his large attentive eyes. He stared down at me from a great height as he watched me throw ping pong balls into jam jars, and I knew in an instant it was love at first sight. I asked him his name and he quietly mouthed 'Bob'. He didn't look like a Bob so I eventually nicknamed him 'Slim'.

After a while, me staring at him and him staring at me, we connected, and eventually we went back to my home together. I always remember that stroll back through the country lanes to my house on that humid night with the bright stars permeating the night sky, and me clutching him and feeling so lucky.

Through the passage of time, we became best friends. Although he was quite shy and solitary, his presence was hypnotic. Never passing judgement, he remained my friend throughout and saw me through many of my relationships, a broken marriage, and the many difficulties life threw at me. Slim listened to all my woes, hour upon hour. He was a silent guy but I always knew he would be there for me. I could tell him my deepest secrets and knew he would remain my confidant.

He would often hide from the world. His favourite place to linger was under a grey brick bridge where he enjoyed his own quiet space. I knew where to find him and when he spotted me, he would appear with gusto and joy at my appearance.

Slim was a soothing influence on my life. I always felt a calmness whenever I was around him.

The years rolled by and took their toll. I moved house a few times and he would always be there to keep an eye on me. Slim gradually fattened as he aged, so I eventually changed his nickname to 'Tubs'!

I came to take him for granted until, one day, I could see he was not himself. He was leaning drunkenly towards one side. His mouth was opening and shutting as he tried to mouth words to me, but alarm bells began ringing. What was wrong with Tubs? What could I do to help him?

'What's up, Tubs? What's up?'

He just stared at me in silence.

I gave him a little aspirin to see if that would help him. Aspirins are good for most ailments they say.

'Take this, Tubs,' I urged.

But it had no effect.

I could begin to feel a panic set in. What should I do?

'Come on, Tubs. Come on.' He was certainly listless.

I went to bed that night with a heavy heart, feeling helpless.

The next day, I sprang out of bed and raced to my dearest friend. There he was, lying motionless on the surface of the water. My darling Tubs.

My heart burst and tears like blinding rain rolled down my face as I gently lifted him out of his fish bowl and lay him on a tissue.

I loved him more than words could say. He had stolen my heart.

I placed him gently in a tin and buried him under a red rose bush in the garden, along with the bridge he loved.

I chokingly said a little prayer.

Who can say who or what you give your heart to?

PANTOUM

ONE LITTLE BIRD

Faltering in the darkness she winged, keeping her back to the rain.
A feathered fledgling stained by untruths taught herself how to survive,
And trilled sweetly with shrill notes of joy, in her softening of pain,
As she struggled to survive in the harshness of the world.

A feathered fledgling stained by untruths taught herself how to survive.
Thrown from the comfort of her nest, into the chaos dropped.
As she struggled to survive in the harshness of the world,
One little bird in her premature weakness winged her way in life.

Thrown from the comfort of her nest, into the chaos dropped.
Damaged by the frosty burns of her parents' genes,
One little bird in her premature weakness, winged her way in life,
And flew through the greyness of the sky, with emotions eggshell thin.

Damaged by the frosty burns of her parents' genes,
Faltering in the darkness she winged, keeping her back to the rain,
And flew through the greyness of the sky, with emotions eggshell thin,
And trilled sweetly with shrill notes of joy, in her softening of pain.

BRIZZLE BLUES

Yoom doggin I up cos I'm looking at thee, but I'm given sum fawt me cockers on all of they ills.

First up we 'ave Flo wiv bunions, shiny like two gert-lush onions, gives 'er yip, feet like kippers, wears 'er slippers.

Then there's Ken wiv IBS, gassy like eem been on Fatchers, don't get near ee, or light matches.

Our airy Mary wiv worn-out knees, with Mead ospidal, ain't pleased. Waiting list's a gert mile long, as an epee, moanin' wiv 'er whingin' song. Dursn't tell 'er it's cos shem fat, baint brave like that, I am a twat.

Dot 'as sticks an' clickety 'ips, that baint been fixed,

but she as 'er Fred, eem looks 'alf dead, as 'im dangling on a string, poor fing.

Poor old Eff 'as 'er 'ayfever, wipes 'er snout wiv 'anky snoee, looks so groee, peepers bloodshot red.

Linel 'as the fickest wart, bigger than a Clark's gurt pie, an' when I talk it stares at I.

Then there's George whom fancies Ida,

Sticks Viagra in 'is cider.

Bill 'as such an asthmawl chest, wears string vest, uses puffer, lives wif muvver, wha a duffer, nuff said.

Kev finks that ee is grand, met 'im down the Rose and Crown. Eem 'ad a duff up wiv 'is cancer, 'ear 'im brag. Tells I bout 'is bowel bag.

Jack 'as back, gives 'im jip, somefinks slipped. It goes in spasms. Yum attle avit, bad backs they'm all the fashion.

Bee's just 'ad 'er diagnosis, macky grapes are varicoses and found out shem got frombosis.

Our guddon granner shem top class, but 'as 'an abscess on 'er ass.

Poor idjut Jim, 'is eyes are dim, they'm says ee as glaucoma. It ain't that bad if it's all ee 'ad but like Kev ee 'as a stoma.

Len groans about 'is men'al state, I finks em said psychosis, but yum better duck, is it sumfink ee ate? Because ee 'as 'alitosis.

Grace went a pisser an' wears a brace, and 'as a gert scrage upon 'er face.

Ivy minger with tinnitus, spongilius, arfiritus. Also shem got 'ousemaid's knee, and its painen to take a pee, pops summut for cystitis.

Ken does a runner to the bog, peeing keeps 'im active, prostate only works by 'alf, fyroids overactive, blood pressures 'it the roof, cholestrawl just the same, ee 'as 'is blood tests monfly but they casn't find 'is vein.

Poor old munter Sadie sheda wear 'er TENA Ladies, womb 'as dropped, need an op, so brassed off 'er casn't couff.

Our Marge always carries 'er pills, shem lines 'em on the table. I knows I dursn't dis 'er long scuddy list but she bain't got gurt loads like our Mabel.

Kaf opens 'er mouf but I ain't 'erd a lot as shem just been fixed with new dentures. I baint 'erd a word when 'er teef slop and drop cuss shem never made sense wiv demenja.

Gashead Ted 'ad a blud clot, a week in a comma and they'm just found a wart that they'm finks melanoma.

Like a dedun was our grampfer, a strong message sent, veins kno'id and clo'id theym fi'ed a stent.

Swellead Bert as the big C, e'm dusn't care, though ees so sick of awspital trips, the old duffer as kept all is 'air.

Me luvvers, I'm pissed off wiv all of theym ills, now I just wants a laff, so I'm mee'in me spanners for a good ol shoo-en down The Bear and Rugged Staff.

CAMERA CRAZY

Beckoning reeds like shifting sands,
Quiver below the sobbing sun.
Dour misty cloaks wrap the wetlands' face,
And sprinkle teardrops one by one.
Pond skaters punctuate the gloom,
Between the ripples of seeds,
Spread on their dinner plate.
Brushes of down sketches its shadows,
Upon the hauntings of each lake.

As poised waders await,
Glued-on banks of silted sullied sludge,
Small groups of humans arrive in anticipation.
Huddled within their darkened slit-eyed hides,
They observe, waiting, breath abating,
For glimpses of their chosen bird,
Coming home to roost.

Echoing calls signal, amongst the blur,
And smoky skies smur their imminent arrival.
Circling, winged ghostly cries reverberate,
And fill the skies, but alas nothing to be seen.
Frightened, fleeing one by one,
They disappear in the miasma air.
In hope camera eyes click open,
In a blink of an eye, lids shut.
Whispering folks with gadgets,
Huddle within the moistened huts.
Twitchers click, click, clicking,
At nothing, in their camera craze.
Who's watching who,
Is the question,
Amongst nature's farcical haze?

CAN I BEGIN ANEW?

The sun illuminates the motes dancing upon your grave.
A shadow skips unashamedly across your name.
Quizzically my brain attempts to rationalise why?
Why you had to fly, and leave me to walk my nights in grief.

Acedia takes a grip of my heart, in this far side of despair.
Another ghostly cloud accompanies this mourner.
In quietude your oak tree remains, naked and tuneless,
In the breathless air, and bows in homage to where you lay.

In the space of silence, I utter a sigh.
Four years since you passed away.
I loved you too much.
I try to reconstruct your loving face, erased by time.

Stale are my tears trodden into the cold unforgiving earth,
My heart has withered and died, living with loss.
Alas today my cheeks are as dry as the leaves underfoot.
Widow lines congregate around the corners of my lifeless eyes.

Can I one day purse my lips to someone else,
And whisper with sincerity, I love you?
Can I feel again? Will my cold shell break?
Will someone love me with all of his heart?

Can I begin anew? My fate lies in the Heavens.

CANCER THE CRAB (KNOW THYSELF)

In the blue-green dominion of the sea,
That rises and falls, KNOW THYSELF.
In the powerful ebb and flow of tides,
and the manic ticking of time,
where the world's madness still exists,
a little crab in the fourth house,
born on the cusp,
hides within herself.
In a crusted armour of pretence,
afraid to display her sensitivity,
she fears the unforeseen barbs of rebuff.
A crab called Cancer scuttles sideways,
retreating into the ruins of the deep,
searching for an escape route from life.
She attempts to bury her head in the sand,
allowing no one to spy her vulnerability,
bubbling below the surface.
The timorous creature, the nurturer,
finds solace in her homely shell.
In her flame-dipped crust she dwells,
along with ghostly wrecks of the damned.
With cracking claws, the cardinal water sign,
fishes for the fine wine of passion's essence.
Tenaciously she grasps tightly to her dreams,

as the curtain of day hastens to a close.
The silvery moon rises upon its daughter,
and determines her destiny.
In the intermittent sea mist of her flirtation,
she prays for the acquaintance of love.
Between pensive moods and briny tears,
in sand-strewn devil-damned caverns,
of her mind's perturbances,
intense emotions ride bareback,
amongst the crashing and dashing of waves.

Alas too sensitive for this world,
This crab smashes herself endlessly,
against the jagged rocks of rejection,
and shatters.

COBWEB

Filigree spun, suspended, hung,
in autumn's morning mist.
Mother Nature, weeping, stoops
to shed her tear-stained kiss.
Cascading droplets one by one,
pierced on emerald blades,
A caressing hush with fondling fingers
Soothes the verdant glade.
Hooked on albescent lifeless limbs,
dreamlike whispering dew.
Life and death intertwined,
pleach-plash, a haunting hue.
Blinking beaded teardrops
Reflect the awakening sun,
lattice lacework, jewelled bedecked,
glinting, glistening, slung.
Shimmering, shivering, quivering trails,
criss-crossing gossamer threads,
Crippled outstretched hands awaiting, beauty baiting,
swallows up the dead.
Hidden dangers, who can tell,
what it is we find?
When we creep through ghostly cobwebs
in the corners of our mind.

CONCRETE COFFIN

Frosted pane, crystal glass,
Sheet of rigid ice,
Escape, my freedom's all I ask,
From this six-sided dice.
Peering through my hole,
So damp, so drab, so bare.
Into which I often crawl,
Pretending you're not there.
Chained within, outlet scratched, screened,
Who locked it, was it me?
Smudged prints around a doorknob scarred,
Prisoner fights to be free.
Possessions make a home,
So what, I bought a few,
Tired table taut, a Moorcroft there,
What difference does this do?
Dial us if you need a friend,
Strong shoulders lent to cry on.
Would you listen, or pretend,
Samaritan, to hear my sad song?
Their voice would plead "Hold on!"
Screaming from a distant earth,
But I feel I've held on far too long,
To a life of irrelevant worth.

Staring down an empty road,
Burdened with a leaded heart,
On my perch, I feel forlorn,
And know I must depart.
Stooping low, I count my pills,
Just forty steps away,
From all the suffering and pain,
In solitude, I pray.
Farewell, cruel world, I've had enough,
A lonely life I'm leaving.
The road I've travelled has been rough,
For me, there will be no grieving.
Taking a life is a terrible sin,
I hope someone finds me here.
My darkened room is closing in,
and no one, BUT I, shed a tear.

HAIKU

CONNECTION

*We are connected.
Integrate and resonate,
Be part of the 'all'.*

COSTA COFFEE

A soft hum of chatter fills the coffee shop, punctuated by the loud clattering of china. An aroma of coffee drifts through the warm fuggy air. A man sits quietly in the corner of the coffee shop, trying to blend in with the Egyptian linen walls, and keeps his eyes fixed firmly on his newspaper. A scruffy, unwashed eight-year-old lad in a grey stained tracksuit saunters across to where he sits. The boy sidles up to him.

'What's your name, mister?' he calls and sniffs loudly. A green candlestick quickly disappears up his left nostril. 'What's your name, mister?' he shouts again.

John furtively glances up and clears his throat, but before he can answer, the larger-than-life mother pipes up. 'What's up wiv you, mate? Cat got your tongue?'

'John, madam, my name is John.'

'Gosh, yum posh, ain't you, callin' me madam. Anyway, don't take any notice of our Jase. He's a pain in the ass. Come on, Jase, leave the man alone. Come 'ere and read your *Beano*.' She dives into her over-spilling pink plastic handbag embellished with black flowers and retrieves the comic.

John clears his throat again and glances down at his newspaper. He cannot but overhear the conversation between the rotund mother and her scruffy mate. There is a large kerfuffle as they park themselves on the neighbouring table. *O God*, thinks John, *please, please don't seat yourselves there.*

The two women glance furtively at John again. The woman's mate rises and staggers off to collect the coffees. After a few minutes of queuing, she arrives at the table, panting and groaning. ''Ere's your laaee, Trace. I've slopped some of it on the saucer but – never mind – I grabbed some of they tissues. I bought u a gert big brownie as well.'

'Fanks, Ang, but I'm fat enuff wivout that,' replies the mother. They both collapse into giggles.

John glances up again just in time to see the peroxide blonde mother pulling her low-cut black T-shirt over the rising swell of her ample bosoms, then cram in her loud rose tattoo. John stares down again at his newspaper, trying not to make any eye contact with them.

Ange, the mother's mate, looks across at John. 'Did you say your name was John? Me bruver's called John.' John reddens a little. 'Yu shy, baint yu,' she shouts across. John casts his eyes once more onto the paper. ''E's frightened to look at us, 'specially not our Jase in case someun finks e'es a perv. Ain't I right, John?' says the mother. 'That's why yum was embarrassed when ee spoke to you.'

'Well, it's not the done thing for a man to strike up a conversation with a little boy in a coffee shop.'

'Why?' asks Ang.

The mother pipes in, 'Don't be a dummy, Ang. I know, John, you ain't a weirdo cos yum got luverly blue eyes like the sea.'

'The sea down Wesson is brown, Trace, not blue,' snaps Ang.

The young lad looks up longingly at his mother. 'Can us go to Wesson? I wants a go on the donkeys.'

'No,' replies his mum, 'I ain't made of money. Read your *Beano* like John.'

John interrupts, 'It is *The Times*, madam, not the *Beano*.'

'Well, it's all the same, just a load of rubbish.'

Ang laughs out loud. ''E keeps callin' you madam – you ain't no madam, are yu, Trace? What yum readin' in *The Times*?'

John clears his throat again. 'The stocks and shares mainly.'

Tracey fidgets on her chair. 'Told you it was crap.' She pauses and suddenly spits out, 'You can sit wiv us if yu wants, John.'

John takes a sharp intake of breath. 'No thank you, ladies, I have to be off.' He takes a sideways glance at Jason. 'Goodbye, young lad.' He folds up his newspaper and tucks it under his arm while holding out his slightly sweaty palm to shake the hands of the two rotund women.

'Gosh, e'm really posh ee wants I to shake 'is 'and,' replies Angie.

Suddenly, a smutty magazine slips from between the pages of *The Times* onto the floor. John tries to retrieve it quickly.

'What's this?' calls Jason's mother. A broad smile crawls across the slap on her heavily made-up face. ''E ain't posh, our old man reads that un, the dirty bugger. Yum better off with the *Beano* like our Jase.'

Both women burst into loud cackles. A sudden hush follows in the coffee shop and all eyes pin themselves on John as he stoops to retrieve all the sheets stuck to the crumb-scattered floor. Red-faced and holding all the screwed-up sheets of paper under his arm like a rugby player with a crumpled ball, he dives unceremoniously towards the scoring line and disappears through the exit in a puff of smoke.

DACTYLS

Vanishing into the night sky,
Amongst the exuberance
Of the firefly,
I find myself devoured
By the darkness,
That gives its verdict,
And cuts its jagged teeth,
Upon the rhythm,
And smoothness of my verse,
That I diligently assemble
in dactyls.
Snatched from my overactive mind,
Words motivated by vanity,
Liven my room.
Syllables, stressed
Unstressed, unstressed.
Lines of prejudices
Dress the masterpiece,
Which displays vulnerability,
Open and raw.

Effigies of emotions,
Flung from a cataclysmic soul.
With a keratose brain,
Daggy and deep,
I sponge up life's vicissitudes,
Through the inability to sleep.
Dum dah dah,
Dum dah dah,
Sewing each line,
My metrical foot taps,
To the beating of time.
Plucking each weed of words,
Planting a flower,
I invest in my pen,
My poetry, my power.

DARK DEEDS

A semi-transparent voile spreads itself across the mantle of the earth and tracks the night. A curious moon plays peek-a-boo in the ghostly shadows of the witching hour. A flickering torch weaves its shining light through the spiderwebbed window of a man cave, teasing the blackness.

'I knew our old man had more than one. There, Chris, you take this one and I'll take the other.'

'I must be mad to listen to you. What if we get caught?'

'Shh, keep your voice down. Now, let's get going.'

'You better keep your word about buying me a pint every night for a fortnight at our local,' whispers Chris.

'A week, I said. Don't try it on, mate,' snaps Darren.

The two lads stumble across the sodden grass and load their spades into the back of the white van and speed off, leaving behind a trail of fog and a wandering throaty echo.

They arrive fifteen minutes later at iron gates surrounding St Arilda's Church. The youths stand like unwanted guests at the door. They ricochet their worried eyes around the silhouetted shadows of nothingness, maybe searching for Cerberus, the three-headed dog that lurks at the gates of Hell.

Darren swivels his head around and tosses Chris a blank stare, who is, by then, fumbling to light a cigarette to calm his nerves. Chris struggles to hold onto it with his trembling fingers.

'Look, mate, I can't lose my job. I had to buy a black suit and I've only had it for two weeks. A hundred quid, the suit cost me from Burton,' pleads Darren.

'You look a twat in it anyway. I've seen you – you look like a bouncer.'

'Great, great… look, thanks for coming, pal, but put that bloody fag out. Let's have some respect.'

'Respect? That's rich coming from you,' sneers Chris.

'Anyway, you can smoke to your heart's content where we're going, mate. It's all fire and brimstone,' says Darren, chuckling.

'And it's great that we've got spades because we'll sodding well need them where we're going.'

'It's not funny,' snaps Chris.

He stubs his cigarette out on a wooden post, bleeding in the dampness. The iron gates before them are snug and the fences either side are weathered by winds and storms. Chris cracks the knuckles of his crude hands one by one and eyes up the tightly fitting gate before him.

'Look, mate,' says Darren confidently.

Darren clasps his hands and Chris, with his muddy trainers, pushes himself through. Wriggling and squirming together like two overzealous ferrets in a hessian sack, they finally conquer the gate.

Not wanting to offend the spirits, they creep stealthily across the grass with their gear in their hands. They follow the flickering light of the torch that shines their way until they stumble across the freshly dug earth garlanded with lilies. Chris flings the lilies aside.

'Have some respect, you idiot. Respect.'

'That's rich coming from you, plonker,' replies Chris.

Chris fiddles in his pocket.

'What are you doing, playing with yourself again?'

'No, it's my phone, you silly bugger. I'm trying to make a call.'

'Put it away, we haven't got time.'

'But you don't understand,' mutters Chris.

'Now what are you doing? Praying?'

Darren watches in astonishment as Chris drops to his knees with his head resting on the damp earth.

'I don't want to be wasting all my time on digging if you're wrong, mate.'

Negative thoughts consume Chris, but out of loyalty he tries to dismiss them.

Complying with the tension in the air, an owl hoots in the distance, which startles the pair and cracks open the insensitivity of their hearts. The full moon shows her smile once more, casting her glow on the damned.

Both muted lads begin digging the hallowed ground, and decide it is easier to live in their vacant head space and not let their heart space take over. It is safer that way. Deeper and deeper they shovel, staring blankly into the gaping mouth of the pit.

At last, Darren hits something hard.

'We're here, we're here, at last!' he cries.

They shovel the remaining earth away from the wooden lid and both lads, with all their might, wedge their spades under the rim and heave. The lid flings itself open and releases a stale odour. Both look away, too afraid to stare death in the face and too afraid to look inwardly at their evil deeds. A flicker of guilt passes over them as they realise they have violated a woman's privacy. But as with youth, it will leave no permanent scar.

'Oh God, I think I'm going to throw up,' retches Chris, casting his crazy bulbous eyes away from the coffin and into the blackness.

'We're going to Hell on a handcart.'

'Is it there, Darren? Quick, take a look, and let's bugger off.'

They pause for a second, letting the silence drain from their dry mouths.

Darren shines the thin light down onto the shrouded bundle of putrefying flesh and bones, trying to avoid making contact with the windows of the dead woman's soul, and runs the strange light from the torch up and down her frigid body.

'No, no, bloody hell, it isn't there. I can't believe it,' says Darren.

'What?' gasps Chris.

'You stupid bugger. Quick, shut the damn lid and toss the earth back. Let's do a runner and get the Hell out of here.'

Chris crosses himself; why, he didn't know, but he was taking no chances.

They work frantically, consumed by the torment of their sins, while using their wit as a fork to stave off the simmering tension of their fears. They cannot embrace their uncomfortable thoughts, which could swallow them up.

'What's that?'

'What?'

A whispering fills the air as a breeze picks itself up from the damp earth and flees across the graveyard away from the scene of the crime. The two miscreants momentarily freeze and, stunned by their actions, are too afraid to run towards or away from their fears. Death's watchmen of the night mock their shallow minds.

'For Christ's sake, let's get out of here,' rasps Chris.

The dark stain of night once again snuffs out the moon. All that is left for the two lads to carry, besides their tools, is the heaviness of regret and the weight of guilt.

The mists of misery engulf the two as they stumble from where they came and clamber over the crumbling wall.

They speed away in their white van and reach the local. Falling through the door and covered in mud, the pair dive towards the bar.

'Line 'em up, mate,' Darren – faking his fearlessness – forcefully shouts, as his testosterone dissipates.

The barman looks quizzically at the two lads. 'What's wrong with you? You look like you've seen a ghost.'

'If only you knew, mate. If only you knew,' replies Darren.

Chris tosses Darren an unguarded glance. 'I'll never sleep again,' he whispers.

'You will when we've finished drinking in here, mate,' replies Darren.

They both stand with cloven hooves side by side, silently recalling their evil exploits. The barman pulls two pints of Doom. They grab at the frothing lifelines and drown their bubble brains in their beer.

The following morning, Darren arrives at work. His boss has already beaten him to it and is busying himself in the parlour, whilst undertaking the solemn duties of the day.

'Ah, Darren, just the man I want to see.'

'You know we were running headless yesterday… I happened to find this on Mrs Johnson before I shut the lid. You must have dapped it down before you left. I knew she always liked to gossip but I feel this is beyond the pale.'

George chuckles to himself and passes the iPad to Darren.

'Don't leave it lying around next time, you idiot. Six hundred quid, you told me it cost. Having to replace it would have been the death of you.'

Darren stands in ghostly silence, staring into space as he feels the serpent of shame slither down the chilling thoroughfare of his thoughts.

HAIKU

DEBASED DREAMS

Daily dreams debased,
Trapped in the stresses of life.
Makes one feel useless.

DENT DE LION

Dent de lion down, one, two, three o'clock,
Four o'clock watch,
Dancers, dressed in eloquent flounces,
On a mission in parachute frocks.
Tension is never found,
Upon their tousled crowns.

Tossing caution to the breeze,
They drift within their pageantry of dreams.
Netted in a waxen sail,
They float amongst the soothing pale.
Dent de lion delicate down,
Prance in fluffy cumulus cream.

Round and round, their white blades spin,
Tossing floss in exuberance,
To the whispering winds.
Dizzy, busy as the worker bee,
Playing their games,
You can't catch me.

Hedge hop, skip and flit,
Upon their nautical thermal trips,
Across the calming azure seas.
Where will you rest your eiderdown head?
In culverts, reins, babbling streams,
Or will it be in ruts of a harsh tarmac bed?

Dent de lion down, live life like a clown,
Without a single care.
Hip-hop dancing, wild and free,
Sowing seeds of happiness in the air.

HAIKU

DETERMINATION

Reiteration,
Each time you trip, rise again,
Determination.

DIAMOND IN THE SKY

My
pointed
peaceful star,
appearing from afar.
Her shining tempting face,
how my beating heart, it raced.
My star-crossed lover appeared and left.
Piercing pain, sad again, bereft.
Rough diamond, knife spliced,
A weary wasted life,
In truth confess,
pointless.

DON'T WALK IN MY SHOES

I slowly and quietly turn the key in the lock of his pristine London flat with a bottle of New Zealand Marlborough tucked under my arm – his favourite. He had given me the keys to his flat two years previously, which was, in his eyes, a token of his love, but I could not move in with him, because, you see, he has a problem, and because of that, he continually told me, I must respect his wishes.

He mentioned he had taken today off work to catch up on some of his accounts and, wanting to surprise him, I had done the same.

I gingerly tiptoe into his home and remove my red high-heeled shoes, which he told me he found really sexy. They are the last remnants of the giddy me, the flickering fiery side of me that is gradually, over time, being snuffed out like a candle. I meekly replace them with a pair of little pink pumps sitting side by side on the shoe rack. I look into the lounge from the entrance and spot his black shoes strewn across the carpet. I try to absorb the unusual sight of this. Alarm bells begin to ring in the silence that stings my ears.

Puzzled, I cross the room and, stooping, pick up his shoes one by one and place them gently where they should be and where he always kept them side by side like mine on the rack. With my reasoning slightly curdled, I cast my eyes around the room, trying to absorb all that I see. His grey Harris tweed jacket is slung precariously over his tawny leather chair – not, I might add, on a hanger in his wardrobe where he always keeps it, and it should be. His tie, shirt and leather belt lay scattered across his ivory Wilton carpet like bunches of flowers ready for picking. This is certainly not like the Alistair I know and love. My understanding begins to escape through a door. A half-empty wine glass stands defiantly on Alistair's polished oak coffee table, daring to leave a ring mark. No coaster. For goodness' sake, what is going on? It will damage the highly polished table. I instinctively grab a slate coaster and slide it quietly under the glass.

My eyes are drawn to a crimson spoor on the rim of the glass that stands next to a bottle of nearly empty cheap white wine. The wine can't be my Alistair's; he wouldn't drink cheap plonk, never, never. As if struck by lightning, there is a realisation that he could be two-timing me, whereupon immediately my thoughts become irrational and spine-chilling.

I am sucked into a silence, which leads me to the direction of my greatest fears, and slide through the half-opened door of his bedroom. Women's clothes lay strewn across the floor. Erotic underwear in red and black torment the dimly lit bedroom. A large bra, like a hammock, hangs precariously over the bottom of the double divan. A pair of red high-heeled shoes – like mine, but bigger – lay on their side on the carpet. A woman's body lays half-shrouded in a black silk sheet, face downwards. What an audacity to lay there in Alistair's bed creasing his sheets; he cannot abide creased sheets. It takes me hours to press them. Her long tousled blonde hair drifts over the darkling pillow like foaming waves breaking against the shoreline. Who is she and where is he, for that matter. Is he hiding?

My eyes run up and down the swerves and curves of her partially wrapped contours. My eyes in the strange light are distracted by something sparkling on the carpet. I pick it up. It is a diamond pendant earring. In my brittle mind, I find myself suddenly stepping through a dark door with nothing on the other side. Intoxicated with pain and rage, I step backwards, dropping the earring to the ground, and under my mantle of hysteria, I silently scuttle to the pristine kitchen. Blank-faced, I find the knife rack. All the knives in shining stainless steel are neatly lined from smallest to largest. I grab the largest and most lethal one in the rack and, creeping, make my way back to the bedroom.

All those wasted years waiting to move in with Alistair, but I couldn't because he suffers with OCD (Obsessive Compulsive Disorder), and now it seems this woman has taken my place without me knowing. How dare she disrespect Alistair by leaving her clothes and shoes strewn around his exclusive flat? Does she realise what it would be like dating him? Everything has a place and must be in its place. She would have to be fully trained like me. I tried, in the vacuum of my mind, to understand his reasoning as to why I couldn't move in with him, and loving him so much, I respected his wishes. Two years I've dated him and struggled with his ritualised irritations. I have become so humbled by the pleasure of pleasing him that now, at this moment, I realise I am so fragmented that I cannot find myself.

Zero-mouthed, I stand. My eyes darken like the ghosts of the night. Haunted by the very worst of myself, I plunge the knife as hard as I can into the woman's back, spewing her life's blood over Alistair's expensive silk sheets. She tries to rise but cannot get a grip of the creased sheets. She lets out a deep, low, blood-curdling cry before slumping, dead weight, where she lay soaked in the pool of her own tragedy. I stare at the tiny runnels of blood running across her partially exposed back and escaping through the folds of the bedding. I'm glad I cannot look into her brazen face, but suddenly there is an urgency to see who she is. Maybe I have known her all along.

I bend down near the edge of the bed and try to roll her head to one side. She is a large woman, which takes me by surprise as I knew Alistair always had a penchant for women who are slim and petite. I try to turn her head again and suddenly her hair slips from her head. I am struck speechless as I kneel beside her with a handful of golden locks snaking down between my fingers. I fling the wig in disgust across the floor and groan as I turn the face towards me. There, staring back, are those familiar wide-open dulcet eyes that once melted my heart. Eyes that had once promised me a pocketful of dreams. Smudged eyes of absence wrapped in aqua-blue eyeshadow and long curling black lashes gaze blindly into death. Clown-like ruby red lips are cracked open but silent. Those lips that said nothing complimentary are now frozen in time. The cheeks where many of my tender kisses were planted lay blanketed in a hooker's rouge. Two years together and suddenly I find another facet to his character I knew nothing about.

Swallowed up in the absurdity unravelling before me, I spring to my feet and take a few steps backwards. Dazed, I robotically stagger to the kitchen, rinse off the knife, wipe it thoroughly and place it back into the knife rack. I fold the towel carefully and precisely and place it in the right position on the towel rail. I must leave everything as neat and tidy as a new pin. Words that echoed time and time again resonate around my distant thoughts. Carefully, I remove my bloodied speckled pink pumps and place them side by side on the shoe rack as I was trained to do and slip on my shiny red high-heeled shoes.

I walk back to the kitchen feeling guilty, not so much by the murder that had just taken place, but by walking across his cream carpet in my high-heeled red shoes. How absurd. I reach the kitchen cupboard and lunge at a bottle. I make my way to the wine glass in the lounge and remember to place a coaster under the bottle just brought from the kitchen. I pour myself a large glass of liquid and place it on the coffee table. I raise my glass to Alistair. 'See, darling, I have a bottle of nothing but the best. Also, as you always reminded me to keep everything spotless, I have remembered to put the bottle on a coaster. So here I am, sweetheart, cleansing my soul.' A strong acrid odour fills my lungs, tears curdle in my eyes. An indescribable pain slices through my throat as I swig back the bleach as fast as I can.

VILLANELLE

DR EDWARD JENNER

Phantasmal mists, blood pustules ghostly kissed, along the Berkeley vale.
Last shallow swooping Cuckoo, to the Fellow clocked the hour.
In the Chantry intertwined, history on the weeping vine, Dr Jenner holds the tale.

The vacca chewed, in quietude, viral were the milking maids,
Squatted on stools, scuffed by scars, the variola infection flowered.
Phantasmal mists, blood pustules ghostly kissed, along the Berkeley vale.

James Phipps, gardener's son, blessed was the chosen one, the trials did not fail.
The speckled monster grinned, cow pox sorely scraped on skin, results never soured.
In the Chantry intertwined, history on the weeping vine, Dr Jenner holds the tale.

Smallpox eradication with his vaccination, Jenner's knowledge prevailed.

Ridiculed beyond belief, the man continued in his grief, beside the fairy castle tower.

Phantasmal mists, blood pustules ghostly kissed, along the Berkeley vale.

A thirst for answers Jenner asked how, a hibernating spicule sow, survived the winter's wail?

Camouflaged coiled chestnut ball, wrapped around in dreams she rolled, in the dying shower.

In the Chantry intertwined, history on the weeping vine, Dr Jenner holds the tale.

The sun sinks low, on the Severn's ebbing flow, sculpting shadows in the bower.

Saga in a putcher, snared, a gambling genius who dared, to dice disease, what power.

Phantasmal mists, blood pustules ghostly kissed, along the Berkeley vale,

In the Chantry intertwined, history on the weeping vine, Dr Jenner holds the tale.

ENSANGUINING OUR HEAVY HEARTS

You arrive under duress,
The stress spreads like a cancer,
Across your furrowed brow.
We pretend to kiss,
Without loving contact,
Frozen within the misunderstood
Ruts of our past.
Hypersensitised, we look at life,
Through different coloured glasses,
I don't want to be here,
Neither do you.
But I need you,
And hopefully you need me.
Your onerous smile,
Blows my way, across life's rough terrain.
I reciprocate, and fling my frozen smile back.
Your arrows dipped in an isolated negativity,
Once again splice our emotional ties.
I attempt to duck their sharpened tips,
Pointed by your own perceived ideas,
And maybe enjoying,
The righteous glorification.

Being too afraid to retaliate,
My lips zip shut.
Linked with blood and bile,
We exist. I am aging,
The increasing responsibility,
May rear its ugly head.
I understand completely,
You do not want to carry,
That burden, as I crawl towards death.
Through my half-witted grin,
My fear takes control, and gnaws its way,
Into our unbalanced relationship.
I hold the terror of abandonment,
And loneliness, in the toxicity that exists,
And uselessly attempt to keep a link,
With shadowy online communications.
Please read between the lines,
Of my frightened words,
I cautiously pick, and uncurl.
Maybe remorsefully, tie cutting,
The healing of a separation,
Is the only way we can both survive.

Ambushed by our thoughts,
The gulf widens between us.
In the empty ticking of time,
I taste the blackness filling my mouth.
This widow expects nothing from you,
But your genuine love.
We sigh with relief,
As we finally give ourselves,
Lame excuses and permission,
To hastily depart,
Whilst ensanguining our heavy hearts.

ENVIRONMENTAL RAPE

Trees, with throats cut, scream

Nightmares chase the dream.

Grinning teeth in gaping jaws,

Sinister smiles of satanic saws.

Destruction is the theme.

Cowering creatures scratch and gnaw,

In desperation, in hauntings of holes.

Impossible mission, escaping excavator,

Man is the earth's exterminator.

Material gain is the goal.

Slithering down spineless snakes we travel,

In concrete steel coffins over tarmac and gravel.

Racing down scars, opening up wounds,

Demise of our countryside turning to tombs.

Hold hands with the devil and dabble.

The raping of forests and fields, don't we care?

When tenebrous chills hang with death in the air.

Where is the toad and the newt in our streams?

Pungent poisons partnered. In silence, he screams.

Malignant moneymakers fight for their share.

Nylon nooses scour seabeds, no thought of size,

Molluscs doomed to die, oceans demise.

Pirates of our shores, demons of our seas,

Fishing rights, law's an ass, no one hears our pleas.

Foreign vessels, mouths agape, swallow up our lives.

Poisoned fingers press our throats,

Garrotting carbons suffocate, and choke.

Emissions of evil, the silent strangler kills.

Cankerous factories breath, belching grey smoke.

Lamplights twinkle in our streets of destruction,

Green belts die, spontaneous combustion.

We must ask ourselves 'what can we do?'

The fate of our future is up to me and to you.

HAIKU

EXPOSURE

He exposed his lies.
Although his lips cracked a smile,
His eyes showed winter.

FLY FISHING

He is like Johnny Depp, only younger, but he isn't wearing a pirate's outfit. He definitely isn't the Mad Hatter, but could I be wrong? His hair, like Johnny's, is dark like burnt treacle, and he has the same smouldering black-as-pit eyes – oh yes, those eyes that brand me with a burning desire. And there he is, loitering in Horfield at the bus stop, waiting for little old me. How lucky am I? My wanting tightens its grip on my racing heart, and a blush displays my love, which is acid bare. Not to appear desperate, I slow my pace a little as I totter on my synthetic red shoes. I swing my hips like bait on a hook. I wave hesitantly; I think it's him, it must be, but I can't see very clearly because I won't wear my glasses – too vain. Anyway, men don't make passes at girls wearing glasses, or so they say. The man waves back. It must be him or maybe I've pulled someone else.

I finally reach Dean, He leans against an overflowing waste bin, with its mouth spewing out sticky sweet wrappers, and attempts successfully to look chilled. He flicks his flopping dark hair away from his face. Gosh, is he mine? Except for a few sideway kisses and failed fumbles, this is my first real boyfriend. Dean bends down to my level to give me a damp kiss. I give him my cheek with the pretence of indifference and he kisses it with salacious parted lips, savouring its flush of warmth, and I know instantly he wants more. He looks really, really fit with his low-slung baggy jeans resting on his slim hips. His white shirt is split open at the collar and two buttons are undone, allowing me to peek at his curly chest hair. His sleeves are roughly rolled to his elbows, showing his hirsute muscular arms. Giddily, I take a deep breath and fight for air as he takes my heart hostage.

The bus to Bristol city centre rounds the corner and we hop on, making our way cheerfully up to the top deck. Struggling with my short, tight skirt, I bounce my rounded hips up the stairs. I give a backwards glance at Dean as he cheekily tweaks my bottom. We make our way to a middle seat. He lets me sit by the window, which shows his kindness.

The bus lurches forwards. I turn to smile at Dean but notice his mind is on something else, not me, which throws me off balance a little. He seems distracted and fidgets on his seat. I struggle to see inside of him and read his thoughts, but cannot. I try to control my imagination. His dark brows scornfully knot and his swarthy skin lightens slightly and takes on a peculiar hue. I throw him a lopsided smile but absent-mindedly he does not catch it. He leans forwards with a pleading in his eyes and slides towards me. I watch him lower his long fingers down into his flies to play with himself. His moist mouth opens but his words have been snuffed out. I stare at his silence. His wide-open eyes are straying off course. I feel a sudden unease. I instinctively cross my legs. Why, I don't know. Maybe I remember my mum's words: 'No harm will come to a girl if she keeps her legs crossed.' Surely nothing will happen on the top deck of the bus with other passengers watching. I sense his discomfort; maybe he cannot control his urges and maybe his testosterone levels are reaching boiling point with me by his side. Gosh, I have never had this effect on a man before. I try to lower his body temperature and distance myself. I slowly slide towards the grimy tear-stained window. He begins to adjust himself. Whatever is he doing? Maybe I have picked a pervert. A sudden madness seems to have taken hold of him. My eyes drop and remain transfixed on his large square hands, watching the taut blue veins raise their heads and snake across his rough skin. Then, without warning, he springs from his seat. His hands lunge at his manly parts in an effort to release them from the darkness. He grabs at his flies, again trying desperately to free the fierce beast. With a shocked expression, I stare at my reflection in the window and find I am blushing at myself. I try to detach myself by keeping as far away from him on the seat as possible, but to no avail. Three teenage tattooed misfits at the back of the bus snigger and point towards him. One of them calls out 'Weirdo' and, shackled by the sight before them, burst into laughter.

A woman with a little girl stands up and, shielding the child's eyes from the corruption, drags her down the aisle. The whimpering girl swings like a monkey hanging from a tree. An elderly inebriated, scruffy man – you know the type that you dread will sit by you on the bus and usually does – curses to himself. He pulls himself up and begins to stagger down the aisle, sidestepping Dean, who is still playing with his private parts.

'If I was younger, mate, I'd deck you,' he growls, like a bear with a sore head. 'Do you need any help, girlie?'

'No,' I reply, dry-lipped, but really mean *yes*. I let my dark space devour me.

Although my very bones are rigid with fear, I do not want

to lose him. Why does he want me here, of all places? He is really overreaching himself. Remote from the happiness I savoured a few minutes ago, I want to get past him but feel trapped.

Dean, whose loins seem to be throbbing in anticipation, hangs from the bar of the seat like a gypsy swinging from the waltzer at the Downs fairground. With the other hand, he dips his fingers down his flies again and finds himself trapped in his own isolation.

The bus lurches backwards and forward again as it struggles down Gloucester Road. Dean, swinging from the rail, holds on tightly with one hand and continues to play with himself with the other. His loose jeans flap at half-mast. Shocked, I jump up and, with all the strength left in me, I arch my body and squeeze past him with my world turning inside out. I want to bury a goodbye kiss for old time's sake on the back of his bronzed neck, but now he has become a stranger to me and I do not like this new man I see.

I hear police sirens in the distance. Yes, they are getting louder and louder. I spot the police car with its flashing lights trailing behind the bus as it comes to a juddering halt as we approach Stokes Croft. The cracks of the pavement smile up at me as I spring from the bus and clatter down the street as fast as my four-inch heels can muster. My heart pounds as I feel a sudden strange weakness wash over me. Left with only a mountain of unanswered questions, I totter away from the direction of my fears.

The police swarm the bus and drag Dean down the stairs with his jeans flapping by his knees and his white Calvin Klein boxers in full view. Poor Dean. I glance back to see him standing in the street, attempting to hold onto his denims. The police are struggling to handcuff his hands behind his back. I hear the echo of my name draining from his mouth and disappear across the darkening skies.

Dean is overcome by an agonising pain pulsating from his loins that finally rises and he senses another sharp pain rattling at the back of his eyes. He realises all too soon he has lost Emma. She was such a catch and now he has lost her. He stares down at his Doc Marten's in defeat as his legs weaken and give way. He slumps forward onto the floor, smacking his furrowed forehead onto the unforgiving concrete.

He sluggishly awakens and begins to thaw. A bright lamp shines above the hospital bed lighting up his face. A sympathetic nurse sits beside him. He hears her voice in the distance getting louder and louder and slowly he fights to catch up with her words. 'Don't worry, my dear, you're in hospital. You've had a nasty bump to your head but we'll put a few stitches in it once you've had a CT scan.'

Dean raises his right hand to his aching head.

'What happened?'

He tries to make sense of it all. He pokes the congealing blood on his furrowed brow with his fingers, as he tries to focus on his surroundings.

'Where am I?' he asks quizzically.

'You're in Southmead Hospital. Dean, isn't it? You need to rest, so we'll keep you in for a few hours, but we need to check you all over.'

Yes, yes, Dean begins to remember it all as the aching in his lower body returns. He slowly removes his bloody right hand from his forehead and slides his sticky fingers down his pants, tenderly poking at his swollen scrotum. Yes, yes, of course. It was only him that saw the wretched wasp crawl out from the leg of his jeans!

FORGIVENESS

Forgiveness is the hardest thing,
That we can ever give.
Amongst the violence, pain, abuse,
It is so hard to live.

Especially when those we love,
Have been so cruelly taken.
Or we have been mentally scarred,
And our belief in God so shaken.

We must hold tight, we strands of faith,
And be stronger than the rest.
Even though we always find,
It is us who have been put to the test.

If we never look to the future,
And in our hearts, we can never forgive,
How can we keep faith in God,
And find the will to live?

God will mend our broken hearts,
With golden threads of love.
And wipe away the tears of pain,
And bless us from above.

FREEDOM OF THE FALL

Between the shafts of poignant pauses, cold shadows drift away,
calmed by celestial echoes, sung in the twilight of the day.
From the mullock of our minds, so raven black within,
we step into God's pure daylight, void of any sin.

Within the solace and the peace of Poetry's silken strands,
fresh waters of hope are springing, in the broken hearts of man.
Love returns to the sorrowed souls scarred with inflicted wounds,
from the pain of our own making, we step from our darkened
   tombs.

A flickering light of hope glows in the soothing words of psalms,
and the warmth of the church candle's flame, brings to all an
   inner calm.
Testing our faith, seeking redemption, our wandering restless
   souls,
search for a kindness deep within, seeking out our goals.

Peace is not found in the hollow words we speak in our defence,
or flaying ourselves for the pleasure of pain, showing we repent,
But in the giving of ourselves to God, is the boundless joy of all,
and feeling his love beneath our wings in the freedom of the fall.

Written at twenty-five years of age with two small children at my knees.

FUNNEL TO THE FUTURE

Sucked down a vacuous funnel,
Dross of ebony quietly bleeds,
As I slide and glide through a journey of time,
Out of rhyme.

A blind, stumbling sciolist,
How can I take heed?
When my chalice is filled to capacity,
With greed.

So disjointed, displaced, with a sinking sensation,
My brain races searching for light.
A differential meaning of wrong and of right,
No ray of light.

Once more down the hole I sluggishly creep,
Escapism near as I give way to sleep.
In rest to rift more lighter than air,
Down deep to the depths of despair.

Have you a meaning of life without care?
Plunging into the sea of oblivion,
An insignificant drop am I,
That hopelessly tries, but cannot cry.

Eventually have I been reset,
You must have achieved your best.
Look at me, you cannot see,
As I think and act as the rest.

In a mechanical pageantry,
No more to say that you are you and I am me.
I slot into a society so sick,
In God's name, pray what makes you tick?

Twenty and five weary years have I fought,
A being possessed,
Seeking true happiness,
Never to find contentment of mind.

I'm a tear in an ocean of sin,
My life is now ending that did not begin.

GALLOPING TO MY GRAVE

The clouds pull their curtains and blank out the moon,
the dark grinds its teeth as it champs at the gloom.
Night's nails grate away at the bark of the day,
my destiny hides in the corner to play.

A stirrup has caught my flat foot in its grasp,
I'm nearing my death; will this ride be my last?
I mount my grey mare, her breath bleeds in the night,
her nostrils blow bubbles of trouble and fright.

Pinned to my panic, red eyes throw their flames,
with spasms of terror, I pull on the reins.
Damnation is close as I tighten the slack.
Are sins my companions? I cannot look back.

I have two black serpents, they hang on each side,
and Satan's behind me, he came for the ride.

WAITING FOR THE SUNSHINE

What can I say about changes? Don't resist them. Sometimes you swim in calm waters, and sometimes the stormy waters are forced upon you and you have no alternative but to face the challenges and go with the flow.

Mine began a few years ago. My husband and I sat in the hospital specialist's office, white-knuckled, awaiting the verdict of his CT scans and blood tests, as he had been feeling unwell. We were waiting for the life raft of positive words but they didn't sail our way.

'I'm sorry to give you bad tidings, but I'm afraid the tests reveal you have cancer in your plasma and your thyroid.'

I had led a sheltered life up until that time; fifty years of marriage, two children, boy and girl, our own home, everything in the right place, and had finally just decided to take on an honour's degree, but then the storm clouds gathered.

Our lives suddenly became a living hell – all of our social life ceased, the centre of our universe became hospitals. Fridays were chemotherapy sessions, which meant that on the weekends my husband had to endure flu-like symptoms and was very poorly.

As I had begun my university degree, which was denied me in my younger years, I struggled. My top priority at the time, however, was being a full-time carer, which consumed nearly every second of my tenebrous days. At times, we both needed someone to tell us we would be OK, but alas that idiom of words was not forthcoming. My only escape was drifting into the arms of Morpheus, which was quite difficult being an insomniac.

Another deviation in my life was what we thought were some good lifelong friends suddenly vanishing in a puff of smoke, as the illness was too much for them to handle. Surprisingly, some distant acquaintances arrived on the horizon and stepped up to the forefront, bless them.

During the week, queuing in chemists for prescriptions became the norm.

Then, as things deteriorated, my home was taken over with the necessary appliances that were needed for my husband and nurses began to arrive. Most times, my home resembled Piccadilly Circus with people coming and going. My neat and tidy home became a hub of chaos – being born under the star sign of Cancer the crab, I liked my rock pool tidy.

Tablets had to be taken at certain times, so a strict regime had to be in place. Dressings changed. Then they found David suffered from hemochromatosis – that is, too much iron stored by the body – which was also very dangerous. He was to have no food with high iron content. His dietary requirements had to be dramatically changed. I had to shop for food differently and scan the ingredients on the food labels I bought. Cereals were a no-no, fortified with iron.

Through the spilling of time, the weeks and months passed by quickly and, through all the adversity, cancer finally took hold and death knocked at our door.

Alone, my life spun around again on its axis. There had been nothing but constant change. I felt my life was dissipating into a nothingness and felt numbed.

As the lonely months marched by, I slowly found that not many couples wanted to go out socially with a woman on her own, so I had to hunt for new friends in the same position as myself. I joined different groups – some successful, some not. The emptiness still remained and when storm clouds gathered, I would lock myself away with my solitary griefs until I was strong enough to cope again.

After two years of trying to adjust to a life on my own, I found my home was too spacious and the garden quite unmanageable. I began hunting for a smaller, newer home and managed to traumatically move on my own.

Half of my family live in Australia and therefore could not help, so I had to be strong and keep moving forward alone.

In the last five years, I have lost my husband, moved house, graduated from university, had my first poetry book published and am still pursuing my creative writing.

Dancing is another one of my passions, which I still enjoy.

Whether I find another partner in the twilight of my life is another matter. That rests in the lap of the Gods.

I am not sure what the remaining years have in store, but I await in anticipation for the sun to shine on me once again.

GRANDCHILDREN

Sweet like the plumpness of the drop,
That flops upon the mirrored puddle pot.
You are the flush of the shying blush,
The peeking snowdrops in winter's dust.
The feathery kiss of an angel's wing,
The coloured swirls of a rainbow ring.
You are the clatter of the chatter,
The sweetest giggling of the laughter.
The tiptoe footprints upon my heart,
The moon-bright beams dancing in the dark.
The ping and pong of a bouncing ball,
The happiness flowers in a garden wall.
The tears of joy fill my eyes,
You are the sunbeams warming my skies.

HAIR

The tapeworms part, released from conformities,
And fall into childlike ringlets I never knew I had.
Drop by drop, they hang and droop like unfulfilled dreams,
Upon my already weighted shoulders.
Dyed to death to hide my ageing,
They await in the greying of the years.
Falling, falling, like loosened parachute strings,
Held only to my brain with the hopefulness of beauty.
How long can they hold onto my youthful dreams?
Strawberry-blonde blood drip drops upon the coal-black mantle of the cloak.
One, two, three, I boldly count each clump of follicles and touch my crown with a fear of boldness.
I do not want the hairdresser to drag the biting comb through the remaining wizened needles of my ashen forest.
What is left, I try to tease, to ease the pulsating of my temples.
A woman must take care that her spirit is never broken.
I sigh and hope for the best with hair and honour's degree
Hanging in the balance.

PANTOUM

HANGING BY A HORSEHAIR

The sword unearthed from the bowels of the Cotswolds,
Is it the rusted Roman sword of Damocles?
In war and peace, we all have a spatha poised above our heads,
Our fragile lives, in imminent peril, hang by a horsehair.

Is it the rusted Roman sword of Damocles,
Above us, tempting fate?
Our fragile lives, in imminent peril, hang by a horsehair.
A moral parable, described by philosopher Cicero 45BC.

Above us, tempting fate,
History uncovers its secrets and repeats itself.
A moral parable, described by philosopher Cicero 45BC,
Makes us aware how precarious our existence is.

History uncovers its secrets and repeats itself.
The sword unearthed from the bowels of the Cotswolds,
Makes us aware how precarious our existence is.
In war and peace, we all have a spatha poised above our heads.

HELL HATH NO FURY

He slides between the silken sheets like a heat-seeking missile. His hirsute arm snakes towards her body, resting the palm of his hand on her soft but firm belly. Kim grabs his wrist and tosses his hand back towards him. Luke takes the hint and rolls over on his back to stare once again at the settling-in cracks zigzagging across the newly stippled ceiling.

The bed becomes chilled by the frost of Kim's discontent. Luke is weary with the strain of achieving nothing sexually with Kim. He has said sorry many times for his philandering ways, but he knows they are just empty words rattling around in a drum. *What is marriage?* he ponders. Maybe when you step into the unchartered territories of marriage, you just have to make your own rules up. The trouble was he wanted Kim to himself, but he also wanted the freedom of being single. He wanted to have his cake and eat it.

Luke eases himself up and rests on the side of the bed, before pulling out a packet of cigarettes and lighter from the bedside cabinet. He sighs and turns his head towards her and sets both his eyes upon her stiff cold frame, void of any newly wedded quivers of desire.

'This has been going on for weeks and, darling, I don't know how I can make what I did right,' Luke mutters, his words tarnished by a false sincerity.

No reply is forthcoming from her. She knows she will never open her heart again to any man.

He slowly rises with cigarette and lighter in hand and staggers down the flight of stairs in his navy Calvin Klein pants to unlock the door. He stands barefoot on the leaf-strewn porch and lights his fag, taking a long drag, which he savours in the silence. The ghostly smoke rises like grey hair sprouting from an aged head and slowly dissipates.

He hadn't known Kim was going to venture to the Rose and Crown where he was having a night out with his mates. Why had she gone to his local? It was the only night he had pulled the barmaid, the one he'd had his eyes on for the last few months, the one whose ample breasts beckoned him from her figure-hugging, low-cut blouse as she pulled a pint. She'd eventually given him the eye and he knew she was willing for a fumble and a kiss behind the steel barrels. In a tight embrace, Luke had caught sight of his wife as she'd fled the scene, and heard her gasps and sobbing, which had painfully pierced the hollow of his ears.

The winds of love had blown wild that night and the storm of Hell had blown violently through the door as he'd entered their home. Kim had been in the hallway in tears and had lunged at his chest with her fists tightly clenched. Over and over, she'd punched him. He'd tried to restrain her as best he could and, with parched tongue, he'd apologised over and over again, but it'd only been inane mutterings of a guilty man.

After an hour of vitriolic words and screams from Kim, and low mutterings from Luke, they'd both made their way to bed, exhausted. Oh, if only he could turn back time.

He now finishes his cigarette and climbs back upstairs. Kim is curled up in the foetal position on her side of the bed, as far away from him as she can get. He flops on his side, making sure he doesn't cross the line she has invisibly drawn. He then settles down to attempt to sleep in the frost of a long winter he will have to endure.

Luke has been ignorant of what he could lose and drifts into the shallows of sleep on his side of the bed.

Kim watches him out of the corner of her eye. His dark tousled curls stain the white pillowcase. How many more times would she have to endure his unfaithfulness? Her blue eyes lose their lustre, turning black and empty as time pauses for breath.

Kim reaches out for the marble table lamp by her bedside and puts his lights out with a slam!

HIDDEN WITHIN MYSELF

A bleak tear tattoo on an alabaster cheek,
Peeps out from the moon's gaunt face.
Baggy trousers droop like sorrows under the eyes.
Hoary hair blows wild and free like an approaching storm.
A nose ripe for the picking swallows my face.
My jaundice jacket juiced with blood spots parcels me up.
Two rotting teeth tails hang by their nerves.
Flapping shoes, large as your pride, grin,
And speak words with no meanings.
Laughter resonates; a fatuous fool plays her part.
I am not moulded by your fleeting admiration.
I search for happiness in the crowd's perfected acts.
Behind their glacial smiles, I see my sadness staring back.

I play to my ringmaster whatever role he chooses.
With lips red as sin, I am his clown who fools around.
Hidden within myself, I remain nothing more,
Than splintered shavings on a circus floor.

HIDE-AND-SEEK

Lucy slides down into the ditch on her bottom, clutching her grubby threadbare teddy, and tumbles into the crispy, crunchy carpet of leaves. Lucy tenderly wipes the leaves from Claude and kisses him gently on his unravelling woollen nose. She stares at him lovingly and he looks back at her with his shocked eyes and blanket-stitched smile. She sniffs him and can reassuringly smell the fragmented faint odour of herself still lingering on his brown tufty fur. Holding on tightly to Claude, she pulls up her legs to her chin, tightly shutting herself inwards, and looks upwards at the deformed but comforting crippled arms of the trees. There is tautness etched across her milky face, which holds a frown too old for a girl of such tender years. Her rosebud lips remain tightly sealed, ambushing her words with a steely determination. Lucy lightly brushes off some dying leaves from the knees of her now grubby blue leggings and notices a tiny hole appearing on the left knee.

Laying Claude next to her, she pokes her wriggling finger through the gap and watches it grow bigger and bigger as she stretches it one way and then the other in defiance. Still she doesn't care; nothing matters. She will hide her new leggings from her mummy, so she won't see the hole. After all, it will only be another secret she will have to keep. She draws relief from hiding in the ditch as the evening creeps closer; the dirt does not show like it does in the purity of the day.

The gentle chill of autumn's breath gropes its way through the undergrowth and pecks at the pale cheek of the little girl. Lucy's ears hurt from listening and her mind wanders again into the silent space surrounding her as she lets herself fall to the right and rolls herself up like a spicule sow preparing for hibernation. The brittle yellow and copper leaves group themselves up around her timorous frame. 'Yes, yes,' she tells herself. 'I am a hedgehog, but I'm not going to eat slugs.' She shivers slightly in her loose russet tapestry quilt. How she wished she had put on a thicker jumper, not the silly pink thing she was told to wear because it made her look pretty. The sparkling butterflies with brightly coloured wings on her embroidered jumper shimmer on her flat, promising breasts. Shiny butterflies, like her, who are frantic for their freedom but cannot flutter free. She tries to hide them with her hands. 'Such the wrong colour jumper for hide-and-seek,' Lucy tells herself. 'I must keep still and silent – quiet as a little mouse.'

Just at that moment, she hears a rustling of leaves. Is it a snake or something worse like a lion, or even a black panther, like the one her best friend Sarah's mummy said she saw in the field at the back of our gardens? Suddenly, a little mouse's head appears between the swirls and curls of death. It looks at Lucy and she returns its stare with a puzzled look on her face. The mouse scuttles away through the whiff of decay, more frightened of Lucy than she is of him.

Minutes that seem like hours take hold. A huge tumbleweed of grey mist begins to roll with impending doom across the manicured lawn. The stout hedgerows standing to attention and marching nowhere bristle in their fragility along the shoreline of the drawn-out garden. Lucy notices two robins popping their heads out from the pruned coarse twigs. They hop in and out of the shrubs, also playing their little game of hide-and-seek and daring each other to step into their territory. The little soldiers puff out their shiny ruddle breasts that resemble two splashes of spilt blood. A filigree-spun cobweb droops precariously from the undergrowth where Lucy hides, ready to catch its prey. Jewelled warps and wefts quiver in anticipation. Lucy wanders alone again into the ghostly cobwebs of her unconditioned and sometimes defiant mind. She doesn't like spiders. She hopes a big fat hairy one won't appear and gobble her up. 'Still, it wouldn't matter anyway,' she tells herself.

The day grows duller and bleaker. Lucy loves to hide but not seek. She wants to stay hidden in the undergrowth forever and ever until she dies just like her Auntie Jean. Lucy once more kisses her teddy, her one and only true best friend, and gazes into the darkness of his eyes, seeking out solace.

She sees the light go on in the kitchen of her home. The back door cracks open and Lucy takes a gasp as the figure of a big ogre flanks the entrance, ready to search out its prey. Her heart beats faster and faster as she clutches her teddy to her breast until it beats outside of her body. She must keep as still and as quiet as she can in foetal position, but prays it is only her that can hear her heartbeat. She puts her hand across her mouth, trying to stifle a scream, making sure it does not escape and echo across the garden. The lumbering ghostly shadow gropes its way through the mist. Closer and closer, it comes. She hears her name booming through the autumnal air. A gravelled voice without a face booms, 'Lucy, Lucy, where are you? I'm coming to get you. You can't hide forever. You must stop this silly game. Lucy, Lucy, it's nearly bedtime and I have to get you ready for bed before Mum arrives back from work.' The robins take flight and the innocent hide. 'Come on, Luce. Luce, come on.' How she hates being called Luce. 'My name is Lucy!' she wants to shout, but dare not give the game away. Dan – she refuses to call him 'Daddy' – sometimes calls her Lucifer Luce and tells her she is the Devil. *Maybe I am the Devil?* she thinks to herself.

Suddenly, a large hand appears and swings back the crippled branches, causing a flurry of ochre snow to land upon Lucy's head. She looks up nervously, exposing her fragility, and shakes her head to remove the cascading bronze confetti. Hungrily, the giant grabs at her wrist, pinching it with a craving from deep within. 'Please, please,' she begs. 'I don't want to go to bed.' An ugly smirk splinters his face as he pulls the little girl out from her hiding place and drags her across the smoking sodden grass, leaving her tracks upon the earth. She holds onto Claude's hand tightly; he is also reluctantly dragging his chubby wet feet across the cold dampness.

'When we get inside, you can have your bath and then, if we have time before Mum arrives home, we can play our little games, can't we?' Lucy whimpers like a wounded animal. 'I don't want to play your games,' she bubbles to her stepfather as her eyes begin to fizz with tears. 'I don't like them.' She tells herself she must remember to put Claude into the toy box. He must never ever see what goes on. She must protect him. *Why doesn't Mummy protect me?* she silently asks herself. *If she loved me, she would, but she thinks I'm telling fibs.*

'Our games are fun, Luce, and they have always been our little secret.'

The mizzle spreads itself across the sky and, in sorrow, weeps. Its freezing fingers slowly wrap around the little girl's throat, stifling her silent screams. She trembles slightly, like the last remaining leaf holding on tightly to its thread of life in the dying season, and steps up into the darkness to the outer reaches of her fears.

HOLDING FATE IN THE PALM OF HER HAND.

Luna rises in the cold morning light and sits momentarily on the side of her bed. Darren, her husband of ten years, has already departed for work. *Thank goodness*, she thinks. Luna did not want him to see her with worry tiptoeing across her brow again. She pushes her long auburn hair away from her face and tenderly traces her hand across her pale cheek.

This is Luna's second attempt at IVF (In Vitro Fertilisation). It would be the last IVF treatment paid for by the NHS, due to her postal code. She knew her and Darren could not afford another try privately, as the mortgage on their beautiful house had become a millstone around their necks. Daz had desperately wanted the house and persuaded her to buy it, not because of the size of the property and the large garden, but because of the triple-sized garage that would hold his motorbikes – all five of them! They were his babies. She had not put up a fight as the house would make a wonderful family home, filled with children. She felt a certain amount of guilt on her behalf as they had already been trying for a baby, without success, for four years before moving, so she'd agreed to let Daz have his way on the house. Anything to keep her sperm donor happy. Now, it seemed like it would be the house or a baby.

Luna had followed all the procedures correctly again, with her ovaries stimulated with FSH (Follicle Stimulating Hormones) to produce multiple eggs that were harvested and fertilised with Darren's sperm and placed back into her ovaries. The first attempt, Luna produced only six eggs that were healthy. This time, only three. The numbers were slowly decreasing. Time was a harsh torrent as she quickly aged. *Forty years and counting*, she pondered. Her polycystic ovaries, along with many other womanly problems, had really let her down, and she felt less of a real woman at not being able to conceive. Daz had, time and time again, told her she was beautiful and he would always love her, children or no children, but it did not alleviate the emptiness she felt. When she went jogging, any mother pushing a pram was like an arrow piercing her heart.

Over the years of trying for a baby, lovemaking had become a chore for both of them. Ticking off fertile dates had become essential. Positions of lovemaking in the bedroom was quite laughable, if not serious. But nothing, nothing was happening. No conception.

Daz was staying longer and longer at work, and, in her heart, Luna knew why. Their lovemaking had become clinical, not emotional. Luna felt he had lost the hunger in his eyes for her and now they just held an absence. She knew he had found solace in his own space. If he was not at work, he would tinker about with his bikes in the garage for hours upon hours. Words of love had retreated from their mouths. She would, now and again, point to the calendar and he would, with a heavy tread, follow her to the bedroom.

Luna sighs once more and stretches out her hand, placing

it into the top drawer of her bedside cabinet. Rummaging around with her fingers, she pulls out her Ascended Masters Oracle cards, written by Doreen Virtue PhD. They are her only salvation; the only ray of hope left. She knows she can read into them what she wishes but still has faith in them. Shuffling them carefully, she spreads them across her butterfly embroidered duvet cover. Carefully, she picks one card out and turns it over. There, staring her in the face, is Pan, the sign of fertility. Luna had not selected that card for many a year. She jumps up with a start, still holding the card in her hand. Could it mean the conception of a baby or just a new project? It could also mean letting go of worries and enjoying yourself. How could she let go of the thoughts of her barren condition? She stares intently at the figure of Pan with a flicker of hope in her hazel eyes. Pan is the ancient Greek deity of nature. Was she reading too much into the cards again? Had her imagination run away with her? She believes in her tarot cards. Daz would always laugh at her. 'Mumbo Jumbo,' he would say and roll his eyes.

Luna knew she was two weeks late with her period, but her periods were never on time anyway. Could her dream be possible? 'Would it be worth it?' she asks herself aloud. How many pregnancy testing kits had she used before? They always left her in the far side of despair. Could she put herself through the pain again?

After a few minutes of hesitation, she rises and saunters to the bathroom, opens the bathroom cabinet, and reaches out for one of the many kits stacked inside.

Having done what she had to do, squatting on the toilet,

she makes her way back to the bedroom and sits on the side of the bed, staring with dry eyes at the kit in her hands. She recalls the story of Pan. Unattractive Pan falls madly in love at first sight with Syrinx, the beautiful wood nymph, who doesn't love him. Pan runs after Syrinx when she goes down to the river for a walk and calls upon the water nymphs to help him, so she will love him, but instead they turn him into willow reeds. Later, Pan transforms back to his former self and, after listening to the beautiful sounds the water reeds produce, he makes an instrument of reeds called the pan pipes.

Luna sits in silence, awaiting the result, knowing she holds fate in her trembling hand. She rubs her belly expectantly.

After the required time, she forces herself to look down at the kit. She searches for the two lines, but alas all she can see is one. She tries to produce, by magic, the invisible line and imagines she can actually see it. Oh, how wonderful the imagination can be. Coming back down to earth, she knows she can only see one line. *One, always one*, she silently tells herself. She inhales, filling her lungs with air, and lets out a terrifying groan, which passes from her tightened lips, as she flings the kit across the room. Unable to move, her mind teeters on the edge of blackness. All hope leaves her body as her life, again, loses its colour.

She eventually picks up the glossy tarot card and stares intently at the face of Pan. Luna feels so let down by him.

In the distance, she suddenly hears the faint sound of pan pipes playing the tune 'I Will Always Love You'. She listens intently to the beautiful music the pan pipes make. *Is it her imagination?* she asks herself. Her notes are calling her body to relax.

Time stands still as the softness of the music slowly fills the room and echoes around the lifeless walls. Luna gathers herself together as a ray of warmth shines through the window, bringing with it hope for the future. In that moment, a wave of calm sweeps over her as she once again clutches at her belly. A mother's intuition! She knew deep down inside! The sun floods the sterile room with its radiancy of glory and dries the tear of sadness sliding down her cheek!

HOROSCOPE

Sheila had studied her horoscope for years. She began avidly reading articles about her star sign in the local newspapers and became enthralled by their predictions. It helped her get through the dreary days of boredom and loneliness, and gave her hope for the future. Luck was coming her way, her horoscope stated. Romance was on the horizon. Romance? Secretly, she knew that wasn't possible. After all, she was seventy and widowed. Her grey roots shone through her dyed chestnut hair. Cataracts were blurring her vision, which left her with a squint. Her pincers were arthritic and her feet hurt in four-inch heels, so it was flatties for her now. Sheila's waist had disappeared over the hill and her breasts resembled two burst balloons that hung their heads in shame. Her cerebrum was foggy, but she had written down the time and date of a local new singles and widowers club on a scrap of paper, so she wouldn't forget.

So, one evening, she nervously dressed in her pink floral dress, applied a dash of candy pink lipstick, put on her finger her moonstone ring for luck and made her way to the club.

The room was full of desperate widows and just three men. She spotted Len, who she knew well. He was far too short, smoked and had neglected his teeth for many years. He waved with enthusiasm at Sheila, but she chose to ignore it. The women who were chatting in little groups spun their heads around to study the opposition. *No worries there*, thought Sheila. They were quite safe. One of the other men sat squatted on a tiny chair like a big fat Buddha. His swollen belly hung precariously over his trouser waistband. Sheila was taken aback by her dirty thoughts. She wondered how long it was since he'd seen his private parts. Suddenly, a deep voice broke her chain of thoughts. 'Hello.' Sheila swung around to be confronted by a stocky gentleman with a mane of sweeping grey hair. His deep-set hazel eyes shone piercingly. Quizzically, Sheila found herself catching her breath and hoped he hadn't noticed. He confidently pulled out a chair, pointing to it for her to sit on, and one for himself. He introduced himself as Gerry. A flush appeared on Sheila's cheeks as she swept a wayward curl away from her brow in a flirty way.

After that evening, the loving relationship progressed speedily. They always spent their time at Sheila's house as – he informed her – his flat was too small and had turned into a man cave. Sheila was comfortable with that, as she loved her home. As Sheila enjoyed cooking, she offered to cook his meals most nights, although she did sometimes wish he would take her out for a meal so she could once again feel special. Being born under the cusp of Cancer, she had a very nurturing nature, which was wasted since her children had moved away to live with their spouses in different countries. Visiting abroad had been restricted for a couple of years due to COVID, so her world had become a lonelier place. She hung onto Gerry but something niggled her. She wanted to know his astrological sign, but would he think her silly for believing in horoscopes?

Days and months went by and, slowly, he began changing. Sheila became suffocated within the icy walls he was building. Arrows were slung at her, which she attempted to duck, because – being a crab – she knew she was too sensitive and emotional. The crab's statement of being is 'I feel'.

As Gerry became embedded in her home and was staying most nights, the stress was beginning to tell on Sheila. One evening, she enquired when his birthday was. 'January 11th,' he retorted with his usual grumpy goat self. Sheila already knew. Capricorn – one of her least compatible signs!

The ticking of time continued, with Gerry's onslaught of verbal abuse getting worse. He had very querulous tendencies. He wanted all of his chores, like his ironing, done on time. He would run his fingers across the top of Sheila's television, checking whether she was keeping the home tidy, which she always did. *Anyway, it was not his home*, Sheila would silently tell herself. He complained about his meals, which were always delicious and prepared with love. He began telling Sheila how tired she looked and that she was letting herself go.

She slowly realised Gerry did not want a friend and lover, just a housemaid.

Slowly, mental abuse came into the equation, then the physical abuse arrived on the scene. She received a black eye for not having his favourite shirt ironed when he wanted to go out with his friends one night. She learnt to hide the bruises scattered all over her body. Sheila attempted to be servile and hid within her shell.

One evening, Sheila knew she had to use all of her tenacity to get out of the situation. After another tirade of cruel and callous abuse, Sheila meekly told Gerry she would bring him up a glass of wine to have in his bath and maybe it would relax him. He could even use her jasmine bubble bath. Sheila always used sweet, scented jasmine to dull her pain, as it is one of Cancer's flowers symbolising rebirth, immortality and healing.

Gerry threw one of his fiery glances at her and rose. He slowly mounted the stairs.

Sheila eventually heard the sound of running water. She rushed to her handbag and retrieved her sleeping tablets (7.5mg). She quickly poured a large glass of Merlot wine and, with a rolling pin, crushed her tablets into his blood-red drink. Sheila mounted the stairs and gingerly opened the bathroom door. He lay surrounded by bubbles. He snatched the glass from her hand, not even a thank you. She quietly retreated and waited patiently. He always took a long time soaking in the bath.

In the solace of silence, she eventually made her way back into the bathroom. With only a candle on the sill and the lucky silver full moon shining its light into the bathroom window, she noticed he was asleep with his head to one side, resting on the rim of the bath. With a sideways movement, she sidled up to the bath and, with her claws poised, prepared to push Gerry deep into the water. With all the crab's tenacity, she firmly took hold of his head to drown him below the comforting tide.

Alas, there was something in the peacefulness of his sleep. She paused and softened her hold of his head as the nurturing side of her sign appeared and stared at the figure she had once loved. Maybe she deserved all the punishment he dished out on her? Maybe she was irritating?

Sheila sighed and recalled her first meeting with Gerry, and how enamoured she had been with him.

Stroking his dripping hair away from his face, she kissed him gently on the forehead and quietly left him to soak in the bath, knowing she could never hurt him like he hurt her.

Gerry, deep in sleep, stirred slightly and slowly slipped beneath the bubbles.

Sheila could not hear the splashing and busied herself in the kitchen. She shivered slightly, not understanding why her shell felt lighter.

I AM A DAGLOCK[1]

*An early morning cough gobs its phlegm, buffing the
coarseness of the fields.
Warps and wefts weighty with mucus await the potential
richness of the day.
Tousled storm clouds bounce across the mantle of your face.
Those curls, o those curls, that spring like lambs with wills
of their own.*

*Eyes of absence, flat as a griddle, dark as drossy sheep dip,
torment from their troughs of ignorance.
Daggy, I bleat, amongst the hills, for my bellwether beast,
lost in the foggy gauze of our panting breaths.*

*A chiselled boot-scraper chin forged in iron,
juts from the shag of your mourning suit and mows
the razor-sharp blades that run nowhere and are endless.
I pad the field heavy as a finger that cannot filch.*

*Hanging around your hind leg, I am no more, no less, than
a daglock.
White flags surrender on ancient thorns, as faceless I follow
the flock.*

---

1 A daglock is a dung-caked lock of wool around the hindquarters of a sheep.

PANTOUM

I AM A MEMORIAL TO THE TORTURED SOUL

I am a memorial to the tortured soul,
lost in the grey stonework of an unforgiving parish.
I realise in the darkest hour I have barely loved at all.
An audience of spirits hover, awaiting my redemption.

Lost in the grey stonework of an unforgiving parish,
angels find me companionless, but I will not follow the light.
An audience of spirits hover, awaiting my redemption.
I wrestle with my unfaithfulness in the shadows of my sins.

Angels find me companionless, but I will not follow the light.
Of all the tracks I travelled, I struggled to find myself.
I wrestle with my unfaithfulness in the shadows of my sins,
as God speaks to deaf ears on this earth full of tears.

Of all the tracks I travelled, I struggled to find myself.
I am a memorial to the tortured soul.
As God speaks to deaf ears on this earth full of tears,
I realise in my darkest hour I have barely loved at all.

PANTOUM

I HEARD YOU SOFTLY CALL MY NAME

Somewhere deep within my pitiless shroud of sorrow,
In the wilderness between life and death's rushing winds,
I heard you softly call my name,
Whilst loping phantoms walked the night, ambushing my thoughts.

In the wilderness between life and death's rushing winds,
I grasped your refreshing rain of words to cleanse my prejudices.
Whilst loping phantoms walked the night, ambushing my thoughts,
Heaven's gate flung open and shone its silvery light.

I grasped at your refreshing rain of words, to cleanse my prejudices.
Upon the draconian darkness that draped my soul,
Heaven's gate flung open and shone its silvery light,
As the air sighed and mellowed to your mellifluous tones.

Upon the draconian darkness that draped my soul,
Somewhere deep within my pitiless shroud of sorrow,
As the air sighed and mellowed to your mellifluous tones,
I heard you softly call my name.

I WILL NOT BE WINDOW-DRESSED

I will not be window-dressed,
to impress.
My spirit calls,
I want to stand naked with all my flaws.
With head held high,
I'll stare at you with my third bright eye.
Pretentious ones that make the noise,
You are not the peacemakers,
or contemplators, but agitators.
We all lie quietly when our time comes,
in immortal death, in graves lined one by one.
So don't tell me how to behave and what to say,
I will not be window-dressed to impress.
My imperfections I'll wear, like stars in my hair,
and your opinions I don't really care.
Save me from my so-called friends and foes,
My identity I'll wear as clothes.
The transformation is all to see,
My mind that served you now serves me.

I'M SORRY, HONEY

I'm sorry, honey, our marriage is through,
To ride free as the breeze is for you.

I'm sorry, darling, I chained you down,
I turned your smile to a frown.
Each link was a kiss, each bond was a hug,
And I tied you down with my love.

I gave you long years as a loving wife,
I gave you my soul and my life.
I smothered you with a passion in me,
And you fought like a cat to be free.

I love you too much to hold on as I do,
So, my soul I'll destroy just for you.
I'll tear at my heart till your wings they are free,
But when flying, look down on this shell, it is me.

IN THE SHALLOWS OF MY SOUL

Not too deep I creep,
Where iridescent blue shoals,
Of past lovers, swim by,
In my thought-filled clouds.

Hung are haunting memories,
Of their fast, fading faces,
High, out of reach,
In the misty sky's gallery of echoes.

I study their features,
Which gradually dissipate,
Into the ether,
Of my own self-doubt.

Menacing phantoms,
Of my sinfulness, reappear.
And in the darkness of my world,
I lay justice to my lonely life.

In my ambitious mind,
I await with fever, a new coming.

My soulmate, my comforter,
I seek you out in the storm clouds gathering?

Will you remain?
To kindle this frigid soul's flame?
Digging down deep,
I search out an empathy.

With the defeated,
I say farewell,
To my tranquil mind.
Where pretence was my only friend.

Return me to the safety of the past.
Let me tumble backwards,
Back into the tedium of time,
Where all remained normal.

The slow pace of boredom kept me sane.
It was a time where I could swim on my back,
And freely paddle, without thought,
In the shallows of my soul.

HAIKU

INDIFFERENCE

The general stood,
With gelid indifference,
At the loss of lives.

INSOMNIA

When the night chews up the day,
And the stars like the pricks of my consciousness,
Hang weighty above my head,
I PRAY
Whoever is out there, hear my plea,
Give to me the sweetest dreams.
Supine, I seek the sleep.
And search for peace.
Each night, I regurgitate,
Trenchant remarks,
That sailed in storms my way,
And anchored their scars in the cold light of day.
Tired with night's grave thoughts,
An insomniac suffers in her womb of darkness,
Frozen within the white shroud of sheets,
Awaiting the intensity of day.
Sleep, sleep, count the sheep,
Count to three.
The lids droop, but where's the key?
To stop the mind from wandering.
Like a restless runnel,
I rattle over the cold pebbles of my past.
And as memories flow backwards and forwards,
I reach for my pen and sigh.

PANTOUM

JAPANESE KOI

Who coloured the rainbow? Who brocaded the Japanese koi?
Foraging forms layered so thick, shimmer in the lap of light.
Lost forever in transitory dreams, shapes softly swim in endless circles.
Who needs persuasion to lower their eyes and see such majesty?

Foraging forms layered so thick, shimmer in the lap of light.
Quizzical below the ambiguous shadows of the skies, their thoughts are shaped.
Who needs persuasion to lower their eyes and see such majesty?
Opening and shutting pursed lips, like whispers in the wind, silently call to us.

Quizzical below the ambiguous shadows of the skies, their thoughts are shaped.
Mouths shoot out a radiance of unspoken words that speak no guile.
Opening and shutting pursed lips, like whispers in the wind, silently call to us,
In the depths of our wandering minds, between the balance of time.

Mouths shoot out a radiance of unspoken words, that speak no guile.
Who coloured the rainbow? Who brocaded the Japanese koi?
In the depths of our wandering minds, between the balance of time,
Lost forever in transitory dreams, shapes softly swim in endless circles.

VILLANELLE

JESSICA MAY

Dear Jessica May, my granddaughter so kind,
Your spirit vivacious and free,
There's a gold thread entwined from your heart to mine.

Our love keeps us close through the passage of time,
My love transcends lands and the seas,
Dear Jessica May, my granddaughter so kind.

Your beautiful face makes me smile, fills my mind,
My whispering calls carry high on the breeze,
There's a gold thread entwined from your heart to mine.

Precious memories of you I keep fresh and unwind,
To store in my soul, like leaves on a tree,
Dear Jessica May, my granddaughter so kind.

Reread all the love in the words of this rhyme,
I hope this you cherish and see,
There's a gold thread entwined, from your heart to mine.

Laugh in the sun, your happiness, find,
But just now and again, think of me.
Dear Jessica May, my granddaughter so kind,
There's a gold thread entwined from your heart to mine.

JOURNEYING INTO THE NIGHT

Deeper into the darkness I run, faster and faster but going nowhere. With legs feeling like lead, I stumble through the clouds of dank mist clinging to the leaves of the trees, like a dreamer lost in the maze of her own thoughts. I fight my way through the warps and wefts of ghostly cobwebs. I push branches away with my naked arms.

Pushing, pushing myself onwards with a steely determination to escape my fears, I snag my flowing soiled gown on the stubble of aged oaks. The woods are cocooned by the darkness of death and the carpet beneath my feet is sodden with autumn's grief. Faster I run as faces appear from the trunks of the trees and laugh at my plight.

I glance back as I sense danger and there, outlined in the silvery full moon, in a small clearing under a porch of trees, a being only found in nightmares, rests on its haunches. It lets out an echoing howl, which takes possession of the air and springs towards me on its long hind legs. I sense its evil intentions and turn to run faster, faster. Stars drop away from the skies, darkening the night to add to my fears. I want to let out a scream but find my voice is muted. Anyway, who would hear me under the scuds of blackness now shuffling across the full moon's silver light?

Death, larger than life, is descending, but can I escape its clutches?

Suddenly, the trees lift their frilled skirts to let me through and I find myself drawn towards a clearing. A Cotswold Tudor manor of great magnitude stands before me and beckons me in.

I push my stick-thin body onwards, up the steps before me. My bloody bare feet, filthy with clods of earth, continue in their suffering and scrunch upon the gravelled walkway, which makes an echoing sound like shingle sucked down the beach by an ebbing tide. Like a ship's sail, my ripped billowing white nightie hangs askew from my drooping shoulders. Fearful, I sense the beast is gaining ground. I have to reach the safety of the mansion to save myself from the heinous monster.

I glance back once again and find myself crumbling as the monster stares at me with its piercing marble-green eyes, all three of them. It has a large bulbous head balancing precariously on a huge black ruff that tops its cloak. Hair like matted dead serpents attempts to smother its mucous coated face. It displays razor-sharp fangs like a chainsaw, from its half-witted grin that could threaten the whole of mankind. Dark blood oozes from its parted lips and trickles down its silver beard, onto the undergrowth. Two horns white as ghosts sprout from its brow, and a long hairy tail coils around its feet, and in its thrashing sweeps its own path through the leaves. The hunched beast holds a scythe in its crooked claws, which it strikes with a sickening blow at the nothingness surrounding it. Again and again, it slashes at the night with the insanity of a poet lost for words.

Frozen in stone for the briefest of moments, I stare in a blank state with my nerves teetering on the edge of despair.

As the dark shadows pass over me, I know it is fight or flight. I take the latter. However, my pace becomes slower and slower with exhaustion. I try to lift my legs but they feel they are anchored and have become buckled with fear.

Through a chilling breeze and the conspiracy of the night, I try to scream but nothing is forthcoming. My tongue is shackled to the bottom of my mouth. My mouth opens and shuts like a fish out of water and silence rules.

Seeing my plight, the beast springs. As hopelessness descends, I fight for my last breath and flay my arms, trying to release myself from the tightening grip of the grotesque monster. I feel its putrefying breath upon my face and await my fate as I feel myself falling, falling. The thing gives out a high-pitched scream of anguish before disappearing into the silence.

But was it his voice I heard or was it mine?

I find myself holding onto damp walls and travelling through dark walkways, attempting to follow the light I can see beckoning me in the distance. I keep pressing onwards as the night slowly turns into day.

My shocked eyes open wide and begin to focus. Through the mist, I find solace in the familiar surroundings of my Painswick home. I shiver as I reach out my hand to feel for my floral duvet in a heap beside me, as I lie upon my cold bedroom floor.

'Thank God,' I mutter to myself. 'At last! Thank goodness I have woken up!'

JUST A DYING LEAF IN THE WIND

Criticisms and grievances echoed,
In memory's recollection return.
Within autumn's relentless biting wind,
As it gallops along winter's brow,
It is torturous, in its devouring of space.
Alas seasoned boundaries are as critical,
As night dragging its feet towards day.

An unbalanced leaf in ochre attire,
Trembles within the fleeting season.
Held hostage in the present,
Its manipulator blows its gelid breath,
Towards winter's deficiencies,
Appertaining to death,
Without care or conscience.

The leaf clings to the wagging,
Pointing brown broken finger,
And listens to the vehement curses,
Hammered into the ear,
And tossed skywards,
By the all-powerful wind,
That has lost its temper.

Along the ragged blown,
Branches of thought,
In the torment of the truths,
A loyalty is snapped and broken.
Short-lived friendship, alas,
Like the wind's blast of wrath,
Is just a dying leaf in the wind.

KNAPSACK

Travelling down life's highway,
Hoping it's not tough,
Obstacles along the path,
Will make the going rough.
Travel down life's rocky road,
Keep straight along the track,
And never store your worries,
In a knapsack on your back.
'Cos though you pray, you can't forget,
The hurt within your past.
It's always hidden deep within,
Forgetting's an impossible task.

Stride along the path of life,
Never weighted down,
Keep smiling through adversity,
Never wear a frown.
If you store your troubles,
And you still contain the pain,
The weight within your knapsack,
Will slowly, slowly gain.

Until, one day, it'll get too much,
And something inside will snap,
And you'll become a broken man,
Lost under your giant knapsack.

Step by step, don't stumble,
Forget about the strife,
Stop to smell the flowers,
Beside the stepping stones of life.
Every day begins anew,
It's no use looking back,
If you do, you'll see no view,
But just your huge knapsack.
Face any troubled times ahead,
And do the best you can,
And if you feel you can't go on,
God will take your hand.

KOI

Emma wants a pond. A large one at that, as she wants to keep koi.

Koi, why koi? he ponders. They are ugly useless things, swimming about all day near the surface with their large rubbery mouths gulping for food. What is the point of them? Koi are just the coloured variety of the common carp – nothing to write home about.

Still, Steve will humour her. Anyway, he finds peace and solace in the mundane, boring things in life now, like fetching the newspapers, cleaning the car, digging the garden. Routine chores are his saviours. It stops him thinking too deeply. He was continuing with his counselling once a week, although he has no confidence in the young counsellor who can talk the walk but has never walked the talk. Everything learnt from books, nothing from worldly experience. *You cannot put an old head on young shoulders*, he ponders. One good thing out of the counselling is that in the chaos of darkness, his nightmares relating to drowning have become less, which can only be a good thing. Steve cannot tell the counsellor the real truth about his past and keeps her on a need-to-know basis.

"Bugger, bugger," he mutters to himself through clenched teeth, as his rusty spade hits another rock.

He married Emma five years ago after his first wife had died. They met in the newsagents where he went for his morning paper. She'd worked in the shop for many years and seemed pleasant enough. They struck up a friendship and things went from there. Steve was lonely and unemployed at the time and was recovering from depression and still taking mirtazapine tablets. He was chained down by too many bad memories from the past.

Did he love Emma? If he was honest… no.

She was not strikingly attractive, just homely and well rounded. She was his comfy slippers and also his comfort blanket. Someone to cuddle instead of a bear. At least he did not have to fight off other predators. Her face was round and her eyes, which held a dullness, were brown like her short-cropped hair. Her left cheek had a mole on it, quite a large one, which she insisted was her beauty spot but actually was a mistake of nature. He felt safe watching her potter through life with her idle pleasures. Emma became a distraction from his hauntings and eventually he married her. She was kind with a brain as loose as marbles rattling round an empty drum, but like most women could make a conversation with friends about shopping at Tesco last over an hour. She was an irritating itch he could not scratch and became a habit he could not break. There were no giddy times, no quickening paces of the heart, but he had become accustomed to the well-worn boredom that had taken residence in their home.

Steven continues to shovel stones and earth over the following week and later lays the thick rubber sheet into the deep hole to create the water feature. After filling the pond using the hosepipe, he meticulously places the marginal plants around the edge. Flying Hedgehogs, Sweet Flag etc. He places the aquatic soil into the pond and the albatross water lilies gently around the perimeter, finishing with a Blagdon Liberty complete solar kit with, the crème de la crème, a boy water spitter. At least he got the boy peeing, not a duck spitter, which is what Emma wanted.

All that is left to do is purchase the koi, which he eventually does under duress. Four of the rather large buggers are installed in the pond, which surprisingly gives Emma an orgasmic thrill for the first time. Steve is surprised by the excitement in Emma he never knew existed. He thought thrills had taken a long walk away from her years ago.

Thursday evening, a few days later, just before sunset, Steve meanders down the garden alone to look at his masterpiece and switches the spitter on. He stands on the large slabs surrounding the pond, mesmerised by the spurting pee making bubbles across the surface. He pulls his wallet out of his pocket and stares fixatedly at what is inside. Suddenly, he sees it out of the corner of his eye, rising slowly to the surface between the koi circling like sharks.

At first, he can't make out what it is and then it takes shape. Slowly, slowly rising through the foam. Cold white hands and arms sticking out of the darkness, attempting to grasp the light, and a familiar face appears just below the surface. The parting lips remain silenced by their sorrow. Pale blue eyes stare with the vacancy of death. Red, red hair flows like thickened blood back and forth, flaming the purity of the water. Steve freezes as he stares into the madness. His heart picks up its pace and he can feel it beating faster and faster outside of itself. An excruciating pain takes hold as, still clasping his wallet, he grips his rough weathered palms to his chest, attempting to catch a breath. He feels himself falling, falling into an abyss. Death has certainly taken him by surprise.

Emma has Steve's tea ready. Where has he gone?

She doesn't want his meal to get cold as she's found a really good offer on the pork chops at Tesco's. She goes out into the garden and it takes a few minutes until she spots him lying face down in the pond with the boy peeing on his head. A memory she will never forget.

A month later, Emma is sat in the garden, sipping her Earl Grey tea by her water feature, with her special-offer dark chocolate digestives close at hand. The koi circle around the surface of the pond, sucking at the scattered fish food with their huge pale lips. Her shallow mind flits back to Steven. *He never really got to enjoy the koi*, she tells herself. His demise was such a crying shame. Still, he never liked water of any description after the accident and would not even go to the seaside, so maybe he didn't really like the pond. Emma vacantly watches the fish swimming aimlessly around in circles. Her mind drifts away to the thought of the memory span of a fish. She remembers reading somewhere in one of her magazines that they only have a memory span of a few seconds. *Much like me*, she muses, and quickly disappears in her fluffy cloud of unknowing. The moment of contemplation is lost as she sinks her teeth into another chocolate digestive. Emma does not see the wallet resting in the silt at the bottom of the pond. A photo of Steve's first wife stares through the fog of the water. She wears a brief blue bikini with a mop of red hair swept on top of her head. She has a wide carefree smile, white shining teeth and a beauty that, alas, sealed her fate. Nancy could not swim when Steve took her out in his dingy – and he knew it.

Emma watches the koi. The biggest one – red, cream, orange and black – she has named Steven, which she thinks is a colourful tribute to him. She often gazes at Steve with a puzzled expression on her face; he always seems to swim towards her like he is trying to tell her something, with his black chilling eyes wide open and his guilty bulging lips gulping at the air. Emma shrugs her shoulders in ignorance and tosses him some more fish food. Steven ignores it and proceeds to swim around in circles, knowing he will swim for eternity in the depths of Hell. He once again attempts to call out his confession, but nobody hears – after all, he is only a fish.

Nancy, in her unfaithfulness, lies helplessly below him, looking upwards. Steven circles her and swims effortlessly on the surface. Everything remains the same, as it was in the past and is now.

LIFE HANGING BY A THREAD

A sharp gust pecks at specks on the barred panes of glass. Rose sprawls on the harshness of her bed that mocks the delicacy of her bones. She stares through her frosty eyes at a spider in the corner of her room, swinging like a pendulum in the draught.

A deep, bellowing wheeze jolts her from her daydream.

'Come on, Rosie hen, you've a wee visitor who wants to see ye.'

'I know who it will be. I mustn't and won't see her, so bugger off!'

'Och, she's travelled quite a wee way, that canny lassie.'

'Don't tell me what to do. I don't tell you what to do, do I? So get lost.'

'OK, OK, keep ya heed on.'

The shadow that swallows the room disappears through the heavy metal door. The door slams and plodding footsteps that have learnt to limp echo down the corridor. Rose watches the black smut scramble up its thread to squat.

*

The cold spring day a few months ago began much like any other.

Rose heaves herself from the womb of her alopecia armchair as she hears the dragging chains of riggings. Is her ship sinking under its weight or is it Jacob Marley at her door, and the past coming to haunt her? The skip thumps the face of the tarmac. The letterbox snaps open its mouth and hollow words are posted.

'Mrs Brown, are you in there? Come on, my dear, the big day has arrived. We now have the authority to enter your premises and tidy up. As you know, we have received a number of complaints from neighbours and we—'

'Get lost!'

'Mrs Brown, this has gone on for far too long. We will not be going anywhere. We are here to assist you.'

Rose runs her brittle hands through the grey cobwebs of hair. Her bones ache with the refusal to let happiness in. It has been a hard battle with the council.

'I'm coming, I'm coming. Keep your damn hair on. Ooof.'

She inches her way through the maze of boxes of rubbish and gingerly opens the front door. The door draws its battle line across the dust and comes to a sudden halt. The councillor stands to attention in no man's land. Her starched white blouse complements her thin lips and frigid face. Rose fixes her eyes firmly on the imitation pearls and lacquered-to-death curls. The councillor in her ill-fitting polyester suit peers over her reading glasses, teetering at the end of her pinched nose.

'Right, Rose, can I call you Rose? These fine gentlemen are here to help us. They will not throw anything out without your permission as this is your home, do you understand?'

Rose nods, her eyes flash with a hint of defiance. Rotting floorboards click to attention. The councillor stands flanked by two huge men in overalls, stealing the sunlight. White jockstraps throttle their throats. They wear large gloves, ready to seize the day.

'This is Mike and this is Fred,' barks the commander.

'Right, lads, follow me.' Mike winks at Fred and pulls out a jar of Vick from his overall pocket, removes a glove and greases a moustache of snot under the rim of his nose, before pulling up his mask.

'Believe me, mate, this is what you need. Smear some by your snout if you don't wanna throw up,' he whispers. Fred obeys; it is his first week with the council.

Miss Aldershot marches in but is stopped in her tracks by a stench grabbing her by the back of her throat. She dives into her large black handbag, rummaging for a handkerchief to put to her mouth to capture her composure. Her shoulders rise and fall in waves as she totters backwards. Rose smiles triumphantly. Rose steps aside to let Miss Aldershot through and knocks into a wall of boxes, which tumble like rocks from a cliff face. Suddenly, Rose spots a dusty blue bootie. She stoops to pick it up and gently strokes her cheek with it. The disturbed talcum rises like ghosts from the past.

'We don't want to rub our face with that, do we? It's filthy!' snaps Miss Aldershot.

'Shut up, shut up,' screams Rose.

'OK, OK, Rose, listen carefully. These gentlemen will begin the clear-up process. They will ask what they can throw out. You are in charge, Rose, I promise.'

All morning, putrid sacks smash into the skip. More and more bric-a-brac that has long shed its colour is slung into the gaping mouth.

Mike gets out some more Vick and pings open his mask, smearing the entrails of a slug across his upper lip. Rose slowly rises from her chair, kneading her head like a lump of sourdough. She watches wantonly as her belongings desert the nest.

'I want that saucepan,' she suddenly screams out to Fred.

'But, love, there's a gert big 'ole in its arse.'

'I don't care; it's mine and it's staying – and also that knitting bag you have under your arm.'

'But it's crap.'

Mike slings her possessions down, shrugging his shoulders. Rose scoops up her knitting bag and presses it tightly to her chest. The broken cold metal teeth suddenly spit out their contents. Steel arrows stab at the filth. Paper knitting patterns of booties and bonnets, priced 1/6d, wing their way to the floor. A couple of soft blue yo-yos roll away, desperately trying to make clean their escape. Finally, the missing bootie shows its face.

The rotund men, thick and strong as old balls of Tewkesbury mustard, continue to clear the rooms. Mike and Fred work on, full of passionate insensitivity. Miss Aldershot flutters in and out, her narrow eyes peeping over her bifocals as she takes everything in.

'You know, Rose, this is in your best interest, and when we have you all neat and tidy, we can make an appointment for you to have some counselling, can't we?'

'What the hell are you on about?' Rose shrieks.

'There is nothing wrong with my brain. You ought to see someone about yours, you cow.'

'Alright, Rose, alright, we'll discuss this later.' She flutters out of the door, her wings singed by the flame of Rose's tongue.

The day slowly falls apart, shadowing the house of neglect. The downstairs is finally cleared. The walls where mould and age have scrawled their worry lines reveal their faces.

'Look, love, we 'ave to clear the bedrooms now we've made way down 'ere,' says Mike impatiently.

'I told you no. What the bloody Hell don't you understand about 'no'?'

Rose begins to scream abuse at them. Mike and Fred take a step backwards and retreat into the wilderness, ripping apart the trailing ivy and tripping over the broken paving stones.

'Miss Aldershot, come 'ere quick! Rose is bloody well out of control. We ain't dealin' with this.'

Miss Aldershot, who is filling in paperwork, leaps from her car, puffing out her chest, and yomps to the house.

'Rose, Rose, stop screaming! Everyone in the street can hear you.'

'I don't want the bedrooms cleared.'

'But we have to, don't we?' Miss Aldershot extends her begging hand for reconciliation. Rose recoils from the interaction, having forgotten the familiarity of touch over the years.

Rose finally resigns herself to the fact she is not going to win the battle. Mike and Fred appear once again and scramble up the cluttered stairs. Stacks of newspapers throttled by chewed-up twine bar the bedroom doors. Up to the ceiling they stand, yellow and pale like slumbering mountains. The two climbers take them on. A cloud of dust scatters, tinselling the hanging cobwebs in the passageway. Slowly, a door comes in sight.

'We're 'ere, mate,' Mike shouts triumphantly, not knowing what lies beyond.

He tries the handle, but the door is refusing to relinquish its secret. He tries again, this time using his shoulders. Suddenly, the door springs open, smacking the back of the wall and bouncing back, slapping Mike hard with the back of its merciless hand and bringing him back to his senses. A cloud of dust rises and there, lying on shredded sheets, is a pitiful skeleton looking skywards with its shocked jaws wide open, gasping for air. A few snaking hairs cling to the skull. Ragged clothes suck at the bare bones in a strange light that casts its shadows on the dank walls. A dross of fallen flies lines the floor and sill like dark dust sheets. The room expels its brittle breath of coldness through the doorway and the splintered windowpanes.

'Oh, bloody Hell!' yells Mike, recoiling.

'Quick! Quick!' he screams hoarsely to Fred, ripping at his jock strap.

'There's a soddin' body in there! Tell Miss Aldershot to get the fuzz.'

For the first time, she does as she is told.

Fred and Mike wave farewell to their masculinity as they huddle together in the garden, bound by the chaos unravelling around them. Sirens flood the silence of the street. Curtains twitch. Rose droops like an unwatered flower, weary by sitting alone with death for twenty years. Downcast, she picks at the holes in her cardigan as the police push their way upstairs.

*

Rose snaps back into the present, hearing the lumbering footsteps limping up the corridor. The steel door screeches open.

'The canny lassie won't go until you see her. Och, come on, Rose.'

Rose hesitates at the futility of the visit but obeys. She shuffles down the passageway to the Visitors Room.

Her daughter fidgets on her chair, staring at the heartless emulsion walls. A short skirt tugs at her hips, her breasts heave, fighting their way out of her pink low-necked jumper. Her limpid pale eyes, the reason for her downfall, are shadowed by unforgiving dark rings. She looks so much older now than her years. She spots her mother and coughs nervously. The corners of Rose's lips split open as she tries to muster a smile.

'Helen, what are you doing here?'

'I do read the papers, Mum, so I got here as fast as I could. What have you told them?'

'It doesn't matter, love. I told you years ago to leave and never come back.'

'Yes, but what did you tell them about Dad?'

'It doesn't matter. Everything was my fault. I should have stood up to him years ago, not you. Evil, that's what he was, making you give him away. He had no right.'

Rose digs into her pockets and retrieves a pair of faded booties. 'Here, take these. They belong to you.' Rose gasps, grabs at them and places them gently on her heart.

'Listen carefully to me, Mum. You can't serve this sentence.'

'Look, darling, you have your life ahead of you. Please, please, Helen, go. Don't look back.' A tear escapes from Helen's eye. She hesitantly rises and blows a kiss to her mother, still clutching the booties. Rose closes her lids and sighs.

'See it wasn't that bad seeing your wee lassie, was it?' booms the breathless police officer, marching on ahead. Rose's silence is deafening. She stares at the back of Fiona's wild head, bobbing like a burnished sun along the horizon of her broad shoulders. She reaches her cell and flops onto the bed. The black blot has returned and swings on its silk, knowing – like Rose – how to live its life hanging by a fine thread.

Helen lies on her bed, hungry for sleep. She reaches out to her bedside table for her sleeping tablets. Her doctor was reluctant to give her any more but the pleading worked.

'Twenty-eight Zopiclone, 7.5mg at that,' she mutters.

Helen bursts through all the bubbles of the packet with her trembling fingers and stares at them. They stare back, rolling the whites of their eyes. She wants only the truth to awake. She stretches out her hand for the glass of water. The wetness of her wounds shine on her pallid cheeks as the moonlight dances upon the bone-pale envelope propped up on the bedside table alongside the blue booties.

In a lonely room, another life hangs precariously by a thread.

PANTOUM

LIFE IN THE SHADOW OF DEATH

In loneliness, can I cope, left only with the frayed constituency of my thoughts?
Death clawed at our door, and with a trembling of fear, my husband summoned it in.
Only time, with its tears, tried to tell what I couldn't face, but my heart knew well.
I stared grief in the eye, and with its bleak stain of winter, it stared back.

Death clawed at our door, and with a trembling of fear, my husband summoned it in.
Anger kept me connected to life as I spun on my axis of pain.
I stared grief in the eye, and with its bleak stain of winter, it stared back.
My soul was splintered with sorrow, eyeing the hunger of his cancer.

Anger kept me connected to life as I spun on my axis of pain.
My husband's longanimity showed great strength, but alas he weakened.
My soul was splintered with sorrow, eyeing the hunger of his cancer.
Life's directions disappeared along the predetermined tracks of my fate.

My husband's longanimity showed great strength, but alas he weakened.
In loneliness, can I cope, left only with the frayed constituency of my thoughts?
Life's directions disappeared along the predetermined tracks of my fate.
Only time, with its tears, tried to tell what I couldn't face, but my heart knew well.

LIMNODYNASTES DORSALIS (THE LORDS OF THE MARSHES)

Two sumo wrestlers squat amongst the feculent swamps.
Bloated blots swell upon the wetness of earth's wounds.
The night's embrocating cold damp hands,
polish the skid marks of olive green and milky cream,
upon the variegated backs of the Lords in waiting.
Expiratory bonks resonate across the calling sites,
pulses beat outside of themselves amongst the echoes.
Blackened bubble eyes stare into the night's blindness,
awaiting dawn's fiery cauldron to erupt.
Bulbous limbs conceal the bloodstained oozing groin,
and the short arms splay, touching the darkness.
No cowardice found in the noble dorsalis.
The vigilant pobblebonks in Kalbarri cool their heels,
biding their time before the breeding battle commences.
Bonk, bonk, bonk, opponents play loud and deep,
their banjos in the brevity of the spawning season.
The Lords watch the skimming of froth along the rim of still waters,
and the sewing of life's threads upon the deep dull mirrors of the marshes.

LIMPET

Pots of Gold? Rainbow rings,
'Round a pebbled eye.
Pores putrefied, amongst baized skin,
Tenacious tongues slobber the sky.
Midday sun's stench, masked mutant face,
Fuzzed florescent chins.
Clogged in the sump, lichens clump,
Seven o'clock shadows of sin.

Barnacle boils, life's pinnacles of promise,
Tents tumble to the shore.
Oiled festering feathered faecal forms,
Flotsam, jetsam hem, vesicle adorned.
Ebb-slapped sands, eerie sounds,
De-crystallised muted tones.
Helter-skelter, to clogged obstructions,
Rattle the shell and the stone.

Limpets fall to thy doom,
Amongst tidal lines there's no room,
For you to adhere.
Ships spew discharge to shore,
Slick perpetrators want more,
But who has a conscience that's clear?

LINES OF LONELINESS IN THE SAND

The sun drops its ripened fruit,
into the space of silence and loneliness,
lingering along the shores of my thoughts.

Attempting to soothe the worried lines,
Upon the wind-blown brow of dunes.
A shadowy cloud buffs my heart and sky.

With the intimacy of each letter.
I tenderly trace with shaking finger,
Your memory upon the shifting sands.

A breeze kisses my tinctured salient tears.
Alas, sadness and pain is my leitmotif,
As I unspool my desolate world.

The sea rushes to my aid,
With good intentions,
But in ignorance snuffs out my soul.

The crashing and destruction of waves,
Follow lost footprints leading to me.
And reads each letter moulded into romance.

Huddled in my misery, I finger each grain.
And weep as the waves wipe out his name.

KATUATA

LIPS

His lips shaped for sin,
His smooth tongue made for pleasure.
That's how he beckoned me in.

HAIKU

LONELY FOOTPRINTS

*Silent flow my tears,
Lonely footprints lead to me,
In the blanket snow.*

This was written when I was fourteen years of age when my husband-to-be had ended our relationship because I was too young.

LOVE

*I sit and watch the clouds roll by,
Why am I here, and who am I?
What do I look like from the sky?
A meagre dot, how I could cry.
No one knows what I go through,
All alone and feeling blue.
The one I love, loves me no more,
I wonder what I'm living for?
The pain, the heartache that I feel,
If this is love, then let me kneel.
And let me pray to the Lord above,
"O please, my God, don't let me love."
Maybe I'll carry on living this way,
For some sin which I must pay.
There must be someone on this earth,
Who will love me with all his worth,
And if I find him, by and by,
I will love him until I die.*

PANTOUM

LUMINOUS PROFILE OF PROMISE

A luminous profile of promise shines, with blessed blushing face,
Voice of silence, sperm of hope, hallucinatory vision of faith.
I gently gaze at your flickering lids as my darkness leans to the light,
Whilst a silvery smoking halo enshrouds your phantasmal smile.

Voice of silence, sperm of hope, hallucinatory vision of faith,
In peaceful tranquillity a church candle waxes and wanes,
Whilst a silvery smoking halo enshrouds your phantasmal smile.
Kindling flame, romantic friend, repair this splintered soul.

In peaceful tranquillity, a church candle waxes and wanes.
Throwing its silhouettes against the frozen church walls.
Kindling flame, romantic friend, repair this splintered soul.
Its star-bright finger points the way to hope and my redemption.

Throwing its silhouettes against the frozen church walls,
A luminous profile of promise shines, with blessed blushing face.
Its star-bright finger points its way to hope and my redemption.
I gently gaze at your flickering lids as my darkness leans to the light.

MAKING THE CHANGE

She raises her rotting fingers, knotted and gnarled as an ancient tree. She wriggles them furiously in the air for maximum effect. I clear my throat and mime her words behind her crooked back.

'Numb, they are, numb. I can't feel a thing with them. They've been like this for years and years. Are you listening to me?'

Coughing, I mutter, 'Yes.'

'I must go to the doctors about them. Still, I don't go that often because they are next to useless there – they never really help. They just give you tablets to shut you up. They don't like us old ones.'

'Really?' I reply, with a dusting of sarcasm, knowing all the time that she lives at the doctors.

I push my mother slowly down the aisle of The Mall. I know she can walk perfectly well, but she wallows in the attention a wheelchair gives her, so to let her play her frail little 'old lady' game, I desensitise myself. I pass other weary old-aged pensioners like me, pushing their ancient mothers in their chariots of fire. Mothers who are older than God and too damn defiant to die. We all know, sadly, that we are slightly younger-looking replicas of our mothers. We are the greys pushing greys. I study the faces of their daughters. They glance sideways at me and a slight smile of understanding passes fleetingly between us. We remain silent in our sorrows, knowing we do not carry our crosses on our backs, we push them. As with my mother, I know without fail the Devil certainly does take care of his own.

My monomaniac mother and I pass the cashpoint. She digs at the air with her scrawny fingers towards the machine, indicating she wants to draw out her weekly money. I wheel her towards it. She stabs at the numbers on the cashpoint, grabs at the bank notes with her paralysed claws and presses a button for her bank balance. She proceeds to scrutinise it with her squinting dry eyes, which apparently she cannot see out of. She rams her bank notes and her bank balance into the gaping mouth of her pink pig-skin purse, already squashed with carrots, and clutches it tightly on her bony lap, assured by the warped belief that shrouds do have pockets.

I push her onwards and, suddenly, up pop the wriggling talons. I cough. *Here we go again.* I instinctively know what is coming next as she waves aimlessly at the windows filled to capacity with temptation. Tiger prints, glitter boots and T-shirts printed with thought-provoking words and scenes of New York skyscrapers. Vociferous with her opinions, my mother commences. 'Look at all this. What's it coming to? I could buy whatever I want nowadays, but what's the point with me living on my own?'

I struggle to catch my breath that sticks in my claw.

'It's all right for you, you have your husband.'

I want to scream at the weevil burying herself into my head and I want to yell at her, *What about my father, who you divorced when you ran off with the man up the road? And what about all the men you moved in with and deserted? Just like a black widow spider, you gobbled them up and left their husks hanging from your web.*

Coughing pathetically again, memories smash themselves along the harsh shoreline of my past as I try to bury my head in the sand. My thoughts wash away and wander to my brave husband fighting cancer. I stifle a cry. I have to be strong just for him and get over this duty day and give him the rest of my time. My emotions and responses have been primed, so I try not to engage in a row with my mother because it always ends up with her telling me how nasty I am and her holding her shaking head in the pretence of being a frail little old lady. I do not want to play her vitriolic games. I will not give her the pleasure to play the martyr, so instead I let my silence do the talking.

I push my mother onwards. I should have left her years ago but my grandmother's words always echoed in my brain: *I know what she is like but, after all, she is your mother.* I was raised on guilt trips and now I am too conditioned to leave. I will not become the horrible daughter who left her aging mother in her hour of need. I will not give people the ammunition to speak harshly of me behind my back, so I perform my duties. Spluttering and coughing in the trappings of my surroundings, evil thoughts like acid begin to bubble to the surface. Once again, I grit my teeth and try to suppress them. I glance around and study the enchantment beckoning me from the big glass shop windows. Goods that buy lonely women a moment's pleasure and are a substitute for love. They call out to me but I will not buy my minute of joy. I refuse to let a cheerfulness take hold today.

'Aren't you buying anything? There always seems to be

something you can't live without,' my mother spits acidly. Debased again, it does not warrant my reply. Armed with resentment, the restless hill of bones in front of me swears under her breath and, fidgeting, casts her shadow of misery over the day.

I push on like a horse broken in mercilessly over the years. The day turns uglier. We reach the coffee shop, the same one we always frequent on our Groundhog Tuesdays. I push her wheelchair up to a table and go to queue at the counter like the dutiful daughter with my purse, not hers. I bring the Earl Grey tea back to the table and just the one chocolate teacake, which we always share between us. I catch sight of her shrivelled frame and sense my irritation by the fact that, unlike her, I have to watch my weight. I slide my mother's tea towards her and the two sachets of sweeteners I picked up en route. I watch her tweak the ends off the tiny sachets of sweeteners with her numb fingers and watch the witch stir her brew round and round until it resembles a whirlpool. She wriggles her talons at me once more for effect. Two long stubborn hairs curling out from her chin wave at me. I will not comment on them as I do not want to pluck the old boiler. I also spot the specks of her breakfast still clinging to her woollen jumper. I rummage in my heart for a remnant of compassion, but it is not in my scripted behaviour and I find myself looking into a big black hole. I mention her stains, but she is not bothered how she looks and, as an empty gesture, flicks her jumper and huffs at me. She casts her eyes around the coffee shop and, yet again, I know what words will spill out.

'Look at all those fat people. I just can't get over it.

Everybody is so fat nowadays.' Her bile bounces across the table and spills over us.

Clearing my throat, I swiftly cast my eyes around the coffee shop, hoping and praying that nobody could hear her, especially the plump woman sat at the next table who had just sunk her teeth into a chocolate brownie. I bite into my red lips to check I can still feel pain and I am still alive.

Between my coughs, I sip my tea. Drowning her bitter words, she slurps hers through her tight pencil-thin frozen lips. Whey-faced, she flashes her eyes at me, searching for some kind of response. I quickly drop my gaze and she hers. We listen to the background hum of the coffee shop. We avoid eye contact with each other – maybe too afraid of what we might see. The two of us hunch over our cups and stare into its murky waters, finding ourselves once again silenced by our mutual loathing.

We slowly sip our drinks and I rise hesitantly, release the brakes on the wheelchair and begin pushing her along the corridor of The Mall. I glance sideways and spot the moving handrails grasping at the silver snake gliding down to the lower floor. I am drawn hypnotically to the moving stairs. My breathing quickens. Faster and faster, my heart and pace, in unison, gather speed. My mother raises her twisted fingers, clawing at the air. The screams of my mother to slow down and the clatter of chatter around me slowly ebb away, replaced by whispering taunts and an evil laughter that resonates in my ear as Satan leans, grinning, over my left shoulder, willing me to make the change with one last push.

MANCHILD CONCEIVED IN LOVE

A momentary passing of time,
A fusion of husband and wife,
A hormone change, my fertile being,
Withheld increasing life.
For a seemingly endless passage of time,
I nourished you from within.
My manchild, I grew, to accommodate you,
Until motherhood slashed my skin.
A sudden stir I felt within,
Your touch a strange vibration,
My child will be no parasite,
To this our crowded nation.

One humid night so destitute,
I rode the tide of pain,
Vowing and cursing never to endure,
That lonely hell ride again.
Systematic floods of agony,
My being, you tried to bisect,
I reduced to a gibbering maniac,
All void of intellect.
I thought, O God I can't turn back,

And I surely can't journey ahead.
Surrounded by peremptory people,
I was thinking I'll soon be dead.

As doctors encircled,
And gazed down with scorn,
With screams, "Come on, push!"
My dear baby was born.
Diminishing pain, I wept with joy.
I sobbed, "My boy, my son,"
As I snuggled him close, the warmth of my love,
Only compared to the sun.
Now, a year has passed since that chapter,
Carved in the book of my life,
I have settled into the dreary routine,
Of being a vegetable wife.

But when I feel I'm drowning,
In the sea of endless chores,
And try to escape through an exit,
But I can't find the keys of the doors.
I stroke your golden hair,
And feast in the warmth of your eyes,
And as you hug my legs, my son,
One day you'll realise.
I love you so and just for you,
I'd sacrifice my life,
But I'm only a mother who has to stand by,
As alone you will have to strive.

Never show fear, stand tall, be kind,
And when a man you become,
I will hold my head high,
And be proud to say, this man is

RICHARD, MY SON.

MELLIFLUOUS TONES

Smooth as a warm spoon,
Unspooling the honey.
Soothing as a mother's lips,
On a newborn tummy.
Like the fusillade of birdsong,
Amongst the rain,
And the warp and weft of poet's words,
Which mollify the pain, with
MELLIFLUOUS TONES.

Your clandestine words,
I long to hear,
But alas they lay dormant,
To my ear.
Biddable I await,
In my quietude,
But your tessellations of lies,
Lay in sugar-coated clouds, of
MELLIFLUOUS TONES.

HAIKU

MERE MORTALS

We, as mere mortals,
Must keep on the winding path,
Towards light and truth.

VILLANELLE

MINCHINHAMPTON MUSHROOMS

Round and round, fairies dance with gossamer wings.
Illusional, shimmering, scintillating prancers,
Weaving magic in Minchinhampton, in mystical rings.

Night's phantasmal mist fondles the scene,
Sinister pores, from spores, in silence advances.
Round and round, fairies dance with gossamer wings.

Milky mushrooms appear from a spidery webbed dream,
peek-a-boo, necromancers, moonlight dancers,
Weaving magic in Minchinhampton, in mystical rings.

The wise owl hoots, and the nightingale sings,
Gourmet canopies popping, are shaking their flounces,
Round and round, fairies dance with gossamer wings.

Surreal silhouettes awaiting day's dawning,
Sew circular threads on the scene, so entrancing.
Weaving magic in Minchinhampton, in mystical rings.

Daisies hide in the mushrooms and sharp swords of green,
Unspooling their chains before daylight pounces.
Round and round, fairies dance with gossamer wings,
Weaving magic in Minchinhampton, in mystical rings.

VILLANELLE

MIND GAMES

Round and round your prison walls,
Willing victim wracked with pain,
Bounce my brain just like a ball.

Toss me high, then watch me fall,
Spirit crushed, am I insane?
Round and round your prison walls.

Feel so worthless, feel so small,
I'm foetal curled, whilst you play games,
Bounce my brain just like a ball.

Pain that's caused, no thought at all,
Roll me in the dirt, numbed, lame,
Round and round your prison walls.

Kick so hard my wretched soul,
A pointless game, can you refrain?
Bounce my brain just like a ball.

You've won and struck your golden goal,
I wish I was not here at all.
Round and round your prison walls,
Bounce my brain just like a ball.

MISTS AND MOUNTAINS

In slow motion, mystical mists wrap around the ever-changing landscape. Huffing and puffing, powder dusting. The teasing and tantalising feathered fronds float silently by the frozen granite face in a dreamlike haze, veiling the weather-beaten brow and black pitted ravaged pockets of life. Everchanging masks of pinks to greys.

Who lives within the eyrie gouged-out soulless eye? An eagle swings to and fro, with feathers splayed and circles wide, cutting the thermals like a spade. Calling out his joy of freedom, laughing out loud to the droop-winged paragliders attempting to mimic his skills, dropping clumsily from the billowing clouds into the bluest of blue skies.

Tears in shades of light and dark trickle down the contours of the face. Attempts to hide the lower view, shrouds volcanic in their spew tickle the unshaven craggy edges of the verdure chin of the forest face, and the swerves and curves where quilted pockets of patchwork houses snuggle into the safe hidden crevices and folds of nature's arms.

Lying at the mountain's feet, the composed placid lake reflects in cobalt shades the splendour of the scene, scudding boats scuttle across the smiling face, sending out ripples of laughter to the shores, telling us ALL IS WELL.

MISTS

Bloodless fingers,
Fondle nature's braille,
Tracing burnt-out leaves,
And bristled fields.
Silent as the grave,
Hauntingly it stealthily creeps,
Upon misfortunate shrubs,
Filching their low-hung limbs.

Disrespectful clouds,
Refuse to hold steady,
Teasing the hedgerows,
Heavily woven skein,
Into submission.
Dancing upon the autumnal
Brow, of impending death,
The mist coughs its damp breath,
Leaving behind loitering,
Cautionary vapour trails,
Like hesitant ghost hosts.

Sleepwalking within,
Our fields of dreams,
Melancholy memories dissipate,
Eradicated by ethereal mists.
Leaving behind in its nebulosity,
Our own perceptions,
Of our past lives.

MORDANT ECHOES

My snatched dreams haunt and taunt me,
As I transverse the tracks of time.
Memories levy a mortmain upon me.
I awake once again cold and shivering,
Wondering if I will ever know the meaning of love?
I cannot mouth the words,
Your wanton ears long to hear.
My lips are pursed and willing to kiss,
But that is all.
I uncurl and stretch my limbs,
And rub my false smiles into your wounds.
You sink deeply into my frayed eyes,
Attempting to unravel the truth,
You cling to my nebulous replies,
With a vice-like grip,
When you ask if I love you.
Hope glues you to this empty vessel,
But still my unspoken words,
Rattle endlessly around my mouth, and sour.
I really want to remain in your arms,
Alas, my love I cannot give, I know not how.
My childhood, my gethsemane,
Where love was snuffed out,
Is my weeping wound.

I still needily grasp at any stray hug.
Alas, I remain the wanton child I was.
A vacuum exists between our two seeking minds,
Where we cannot connect.
Your doubt is a passion that circles the Heavens.
Is there no end to our misery?
Words of no good, just trouble,
To survive them I hid in my bubble.
Transpersonal psychology, will I understand?
Travelling from my deepest wounds,
To the most transcendent capacity of my consciousness.
Alas my love cannot be demanded.
Maybe it is a gift I can tenderly give,
if I push through the pain,
And silence the mordant echoes,
Of the matriarch's cavilling and stinging voice.

MOTHER OF MINE

You made me desperate, O mother of mine,
I held out my hand, but you were blind.
A little girl waited so desperately,
For a crumb of your love, but you could not see.
She waited for hugs, and clung to your side,
But you never heard her when she cried.

MR AND MRS

Lingering perfume in a candlelit room,
an evening to always remember.
Soft summer days, on silken corn laid,
and cuddled by fires in December.
A violin sang as I touched your hand,
and plucked at the strings of our hearts.
Far distant plans, made in paradise lands,
on a slow boat of love to depart.
We gazed at skies where drifting dreams glide,
looking through rose-tinted glasses.
In winged slippers, we sailed through clouds soft and pale,
where worries dissolved into ashes.
All time stood still, we two on a hill,
hearing peals of faint silver bells,
that echoed on high, then dipped in the sky,
to rest in moss-covered dells.
A bud picked so tender to always remember,
a stroll down Memory Lane.
Pressed between pages, so yellow and aged,
a token to always remain.
Our names we carved on blossom tree large,
that showered us with pink snow.
The magic of this all sealed with a kiss,
showed you how I loved you so.

Valentine's cards with delicate hearts,
told us of our feelings.
Dancing so near until dawn reappeared,
which sent our giddy heads reeling.

Alone here I write, long into the night,
I feel a happiness tear,
slide down my cheek and fall to this sheet,
as I think of my man so dear.
All of these things are glass beads on a string,
linking us closely together,
and now life is through, and I had to leave you,
my love will go on forever.

MY AUNT RITA

If only you and I,
Could brush the azure sky,
And polish clouds as they roll by.
If only.

If only you and I,
Could buff the cobwebs, lowly slung,
And bring such solace with the sun.
If only.

If only you and I,
With buckets wash the babbling streams,
And make the waters sweet and clean.
If only.

If only you and I,
Could hug each creature great and small,
And paint a smile upon them all.
If only.

When I see the brightest star,
Sparkling in the Heavens afar,
Spreading light upon our land,
I know, Rita, you are there with a golden duster in your hand.

MY AUTUMNAL WETLAND WORLD

Mellow veil on melancholy vale, ghostly phantoms linger,
fondling mists, softly kiss, the Severn's snaking fingers.
Shuddering woven sultry reeds spike the sobbing rays,
Wide-mouthed poaching putchers lay, submerged in sullied clay.

Whispering trees shed russet leaves, Old Spots on the Pippin munch.
Snuffling spicule hedgehogs shuffle, feeding on fattened slugs, crunch.
Webbed, warts and wefts, jewelled hung, silken spun,
wrapped in hope, cobwebs of dreams, drying in the dying of the sun.

A shallow flighted cuckoo beneath the bower, clocks the fading hour.
Bewick swans unzip the wetlands with their pinions of power.
Squawking sinister satanic crows scar the lowlands' dripping face.
The mantle of cream pustule homes, on the Cotswolds' brow, embrace.

Amongst gathered harvests in quietude, watchful chew the cow and doe.
Weary hedgerows, heavy hung, hold dew-soaked berries and inky sloes.
Fairy-tale Tudor castles soar and cast their shadows on the ley.
Clandestine towers peep, half-hidden, in the snuffing out of day.

Brindled, blurred amongst the mist, swiftly ebbs the Severn tide,
Run pheasant run, my rustic suns, over flooded fields, nowhere to hide.
A joyful tear leaves its mark upon my dust-pale face.
God has plucked my stony heart, and in this wetland world has placed.

PANTOUM

MY DISTANT SON (IN AUSTRALIA)

On a burnt-out screen, I espy the dying by the glazing of your eyes.
Clutching at the nothingness of night, searching for the resurrection of hope,
Over ten thousand miles of frozen smiles, I patiently wait with hands outstretched.
In a tear-stained world that holds its own counsel, my mind is furnished with fear.

Clutching at the nothingness of night, searching for the resurrection of hope,
How I long to erase, with my lava of love, the shadows settling on your distant face.
In a tear-stained world that holds its own counsel, my mind is furnished with fear.
Near and far, we are joined as one, bound by the madness of our senseless words.

How I long to erase, with my lava of love, the shadows settling on your distant face.

This mother grieves for her toiling son, ingrained with the barbarities of life.

Near and far, we are joined as one, bound by the madness of our senseless words.

My dearest son, I will always be here, lingering in the loneliness of the creeping hour.

This mother grieves for her toiling son, ingrained with the barbarities of life.

On a burnt-out screen, I espy the dying by the glazing of your eyes.

My dearest son, I will always be here, lingering in the loneliness of the creeping hour.

Over ten thousand miles of frozen smiles, I patiently wait with hands outstretched.

MY FATHER

He was the fading of the day,
he was the echo far away.
No blinking of the dusty eye,
a vacant stare in a greying sky.

He was not deep like oceans wide,
we lived in the shallows of the tide.
He was the dent de lion clock,
he was the disappearing sock.

Skin-deep pockets love slipped through,
his tightness was a new school shoe.
Soft hugs a fingertip away,
were lost in brief wafts of decay.

A hoary crown cropped so severe,
his whistling aid ate up his ear.
A bulbous nose sorrowed his face,
his hollow grin slid out of place.

Clothes in boredom shone with age,
his jacket bland in biscuit beige.
A lonely voice that no one heard,
No pity for the dying bird.

Two sugars in his cup of tea,
I didn't know him. He didn't know me.

MY WORLD OF MANY COLOURS

Give me a world, O Lord,
A ball of crimson hue.
Pulsating with a heart of love,
A soul bequeathed to you.

Give me a world, my saviour,
A sphere of smiling yellow.
Filled with sparkling laughter,
Forgiveness sweet and mellow.

Give me a world, my father,
A globe so crisp and white.
Flowing with compassion,
Which over rules all spite.

Give me a world, my Heavenly Christ,
An orb of many colours.
And bestow to me a heart of gold,
And a hand to help all others.

MY WORRIED BROW

He carved his name upon my brow,
he dug each trench with cold harsh hoe.
I cannot please, I know not how?
With hardened heart, I feel so low.

He dug each trench with cold harsh hoe,
deep lines are carved upon my face.
With hardened heart, I feel so low,
he taught me how to know my place.

Deep lines are carved upon my face,
the lines of sadness etched so deep.
He taught me how to know my place,
my nightmares stalk my restless sleep.

The lines of sadness etched so deep,
he carved his name upon my brow.
My nightmares stalk my restless sleep,
I cannot please, I know not how.

HAIKU

NIGHT'S TORMENT

In my night's torment,
The winter of discontent,
Creeps chillingly on.

NUMBER OF THE BEAST

Adele focuses on the full moon shining through the grubby hospital window. It quietly smiled at her with a dark secret Adele had yet to discover. A rogue cloud scurried across the moon's face between her contractions. She must stay focused, Adele told herself.

The long torture of the delayed birth continued. Each hour, Adele travelled along the agonising path of pain with the spasms getting stronger and stronger. Her horrendous howls rattled down the corridors of the Gloucester Maternity Hospital. Her dignity was abandoned at the hospital entrance and she became only a name scratched on a chalkboard.

"OK, love, we are there now. Ten centimetres, so you can start pushing," chirruped an enthusiastic nurse, smug in the knowledge that she was not the one laying there on the bed, only a spectator.

Adele's wails reverberated through the night and cowered in the corners of her room. The terror of childbirth had taken its grip.

Surely it was not normal to feel this amount of pain, she told herself. Her wide-apart legs trembled with fear and she wondered if her spine had snapped. Adele held onto the gas and air with a vice-like grip as if her life depended on it. She sucked at the contraption, but all it managed to do was make silly grunting noises.

Doctors and midwives gathered around her bedside, deciding what to do. She had been pushing for over an hour. It was too late for her to have an epidural, so that was it. She had to walk the path of pain alone.

The father was a one-night stand. A dark, mysterious stranger she had met in her local pub, who appeared from nowhere and then vanished into the blanket of the dark. She had fallen for his shiny black hair, his dark piercing eyes that held the coldness of winter and his wide-open grin, which was shaped for sin. Adele remembered the kiss – the kiss that bit into her neck and drew a warm trickle of berry-coloured blood that crept onto the collar of her starched white blouse.

Adele pushed with all of her might, but the baby was not coming. Again and again, she tried, gritting her teeth. Her screams became louder and longer, and her red face screwed up. Her cheeks inflated, looking like a balloon ready to burst, and beads of sweat glistened in the furrowed frown upon her brow.

Making no headway, Adele was told the baby was stuck fast in the birth canal and forceps would have to be used.

Adele had reached the climax of endurance and convinced herself that she and her baby would not survive. "We are going to die," she called out through gritted teeth, but the newly arrived doctor ignored her anguish as he pushed the curved steel instrument of torture inside the neck of her womb and then pulled with force. An unbearable suffering took hold of Adele, who was too exhausted to weep. Her final death cry filled the room and, in the chaos of the night, with one long lingering push and the doctor pulling, her baby was born. She heard its lusty howl, but all she felt was the sheer relief that he was out and she was in one piece. The nurses swaddled the infant in a sheet and passed him to Adele, cooing continually how beautiful he was, and what a brilliant job Adele had done giving birth. Adele knew that they must say that to all the dazed mothers.

Adele glanced at the wrinkled baby staring up at her. She shivered slightly in the heat of her room, but did not know why. She stared into his eyes. He stared back with a blackness that drained her soul. She sucked at the air to compose herself and attempted to put her imagination to bed. She shuddered as fear grabbed at her heart again. Streaks of blood and vernix still covered his cone-shaped head, which she carefully traced with her hand. His pink arms flayed, as if shaking hands with the menacing group of shadows that had amassed in her room. His head swivelled around with his mouth wildly opening and shutting, searching for sustenance. He grunted as if trying to say something, but Adele knew there was no way the creature was going to latch onto her tender breasts that continually leaked.

Exhausted, Adele held him close and mechanically attempted to bond with him. Once again, she willed herself to stare into his eyes, praying for her maternal instincts to take hold. There was no sudden rush of love and tenderness. Nothing. She sensed nothing at all, just a mind-blowing numbness. Maybe her hormones were all over the place. Adele felt an urgency for one of the nurses to snatch him from her and called out for help, but they were preoccupied with other duties.

What was wrong with her? She felt a gripping panic and a sudden sense of impending doom.

Adele noticed the moon had appeared again from behind the clouds, now bigger and more dangerous. She watched it cast its mischievous strange light upon her and the baby.

Adele had chosen her son's name many months ago. She was going to call him 'Damien'.

Adele began to wipe the final streak of vernix from Damien's head. She suddenly took a large breath and howled deeper and longer than she had during the birth. Her blood ran cold. There it was, his birthmark. Damned from here to eternity, there it was for all to see: 666.

The midwives rushed to Adele's bedside but were lost in the maze of her blood-curdling echoes.

She let out another high-pitched shriek and, trapped under the tower of terror looming precariously over her, she watched as the night's black agents slowly appeared and congregated beside her bed.

NUMBERS

"Nine," he snaps. "Got that?"

"Yes," I sigh as I give him a sideways glance.

I notice his pallor. A bead of sweat trickles down his marbled forehead as he steps behind me to reach the other side of the recess.

"Eight. Blast it. Right, May, shove it along a little. I shall be glad to finish this, but what bloody annoys me is your list of jobs never decreases. You just keep adding to it. After this, hopefully I'll be down to four."

I obey and ask, wearily, when I can put the shelf down. My arms begin to ache and my knees buckle slightly.

"I didn't mean for you to start my list this morning. You should not have changed your plans and should have gone to golf as you originally wanted. You know it relaxes you and you seem so tense."

He doesn't toss me a reply but snaps his Stanley steel tape measure back with a sigh of relief, takes the 2H pencil stub from behind his ear and marks my flocked magnolia wall. His shadow looms above me like a thundercloud.

I notice the ashen hairs waving at me from the comforting warmth of wax in his ears. The bushy eyebrows, peppered with grey, remain knotted. His hard, dark eyes are splintered with flecks of stone, and there lies a steely determination in the grimace stamped upon his face.

"Right, you can put the shelf carefully against the wall. *Carefully*," he reiterates, like a schoolmaster talking down to his pupil.

He righteously reminds me that it was me who wanted a bookshelf in the recess, not him. Nothing is ever him. He is so bloody perfect. I call him Peter Perfect, much to his annoyance.

"I'm going upstairs if you don't want me," I soberly reply, giving myself permission to leave.

He doesn't answer. I mount the stairs to our bedroom as the clock in the hall strikes quarter past twelve. The echoes roll and each strike crawls its way up the cold walls. I pick up the ironing from my bed, which I had finished in the morning. Three of Pete's shirts and five towels. I seek solace in the peacefulness of my space. The silence is pierced by the occasional buzz of the drill downstairs.

Suddenly, I hear a cry. He calls out "May!" with an urgency, but it has a sharp edge and I do not want to leave my solitude. He will have to do without me for once. I will not be ambushed, I tell myself.

I know inwardly he doesn't really want me. He has never really wanted me. Putting up the bookshelf was the nearest I had been to him for years. It spooned up loving memories that had long been mislaid amongst the brittleness of life. I slowly put the ironing away and, one by one, descend the stairs.

I spot his frame laying on the dusty Axminster. His drill, like a pulled gun from a holster, lays by his side. His eyes are slammed shut. "Pete!", I yell through my desperate lips. I rush to his side, calling his name again and again, and shake him. I focus my eyes on the large shape before me with his mouth open like a landed fish, and immediately I know I am staring death in the face. I run to the land line, as for a split second I could not remember where my damn mobile was – and, anyway, I probably hadn't charged it.

I tap 999. "Ambulance, for God's sake! I think my husband's having a heart attack or something!"

I listen intently to what they are telling me and race back to his side. With hands together, I compress his chest as told. One, two three, four; one, two, three, four. On and on, I pump. Ten minutes later, I hear the siren. I rush to let them in and step backwards to let them do their business. Twenty minutes later, I could tell by their expressions and the smouldering stillness of the room that he had gone. The paramedics uneasily searched for comforting words that collapsed under their weight.

With my reasoning torn, I bend to kiss his weathered hands and notice the dirt under his cracked nails. Hands that had toiled hard to please me.

The clock strikes one – the lonely hour. The silent steps of time plod steadily forward.

A strange light feeds upon the cold landscape and returns my empty stare. He was a solitary man. Will he be remembered in years to come by anybody else but me? The shelf remains upright against the magnolia wall like a gravestone with an invisible epitaph: 'He should never have changed his plans'.

O, MIRROR, MIRROR ON THE WALL

Stone-faced stare,
no life there.
Deeply lined,
passage of time.
Glancing slanted, all in vain,
at empty eyes concealing pain.

Hopes hung hazy in the mist,
dying dreams by death's chilled kiss.
All that's seen, not as it seems,
tightened lips in silence scream.
Is it really me stood there?
Reflected, ghostly, haunting stare.

Chiselled, creviced face ground down,
who carved the furrowed frown?
O mirror, mirror on the wall,
hide deep the secrets of my soul.
Maybe it was I,
who glazed the lifeless eyes?

Where is the girl with the smiling face?
Listless eyes stare into space.
Where are you, Julie? I implore.
Glass splinters glisten on the floor.
Life's bloody sap seeps from gnarled hands.
Through channels of years, soft tears flow down.

OLD GREY LADY

Old grey lady, seeking solace, high on a scraggy hill,
You love to watch the clouds roll by, but hide away you will.
So lonely but you refuse all help, afraid, why do we pry?
You whisper, 'Let them leave me alone to gaze into the sky.
I want no more of this desperate life with its frightening maniac pace,
No more of the gossip, whispers and scorns thrown at me by my own race.'

O, old grey lady in solitude stands, perched against the heavens above,
The wind, the rain, the fields, the trees, are these your only loves?
Your youth has left you, your beauty etiolated, only the lines remain,
To relate all the laughter, the fun you once had, and also the bad times and pain.
Hair so ashen, hung limp of life, has it ever seen a comb,
A threadbare coat tightly bound. O tell me, where is your home?
Old grey lady, like death you stand for eternity it seems,
No being should ever encroach on you, lost in the web of your dreams.
So much you could tell of the years that rolled by, your dreams did you ever fulfil?

The woman I see, is it a reflection of me, gazing out on a desolate hill.

OLD MOTHER HUBBARD

Pat Hubbard clutches with one deformed hand the yellowing net curtains and glances out of the window. She runs her other icy fingers along the sill, searching for any lost pills.

She watches the greyness as heavy as grief drop upon the adjoining park. Tufts of damp grass, in their wilderness, keep their heads unbowed. Rose bushes hacked mercilessly to within an inch of their lives threaten the passers-by with their armoury of swords. Like military men on parade, they line the shiny well-trodden paths that go nowhere in particular.

'What are you gawping at?' snaps Colin with frosty words.

'Nothing, just checking the weather.'

Pat, knowing when to zip her lip, silently stares into the abyss through the condensation dribbling down her kitchen windowpane.

'Let's have our tea and put that blasted curtain down,' yells Colin in his authoritarian voice. Pat obeys.

'What food have we got tonight?'

'Beans on toast,' she replies, renting out her ear.

'What, again? That's all we ever have nowadays. I'll be trumpeting out of my ass all night.'

'All right, Col, pipe down. At least it's one of your five a day. Anyway, if you gave me more…'

'What?'

'Never mind.'

Pat, clutching at her hip, screws herself into the unforgiving dining chair and groans.

'This flat is too damp for me. Look at that mildew growing in the corner of this bloody room. It looks like I'm harvesting mushrooms. One day, Col, it's going to swallow me up whole.'

'I can hope,' whispers Colin sarcastically.

'And it's making my arthritis worse.'

The fuggy air hangs heavy in the kitchen, exhausted by the evening's dull routine.

'Do you know where my tablet box is? I can't keep count of what I'm taking, with all these new-fangled ways of obtaining my tablets – what with repeat prescription forms and now this ordering service, which is always engaged. I'm sick of listening to tunes. Thank God we don't own a computer to make matters worse. Why can't it be like it used to be? Go to the doctors and he gives you your slip of paper. Simple. Now I've got mountains of tablets, oxycodone, fentanyl and more of the buggers. I'm so confused.'

'Well, it doesn't take much to confuse you,' pipes up Colin with spiteful sarcasm.

Worn out by hostility, Pat, in her convenient deafness, flatly replies, 'I've been given painkillers by the ton, tablets to knock me out at night, antidepressants, and I still have some morphine somewhere from the last bad bout of pain I had. Do you know where it is?'

'No, no, now shut up and let's eat our blasted beans in peace.'

Pat rises and struggles to the kitchen cupboard. She opens the doors with her withered talons and plays draughts with a few tins of beans and processed peas, shifting them diagonally back and forth. She grabs at handfuls of paperwork, which has been stuffed in corners. Pat discovers a comb, still clutching grey hairs, and all sorts of miscellaneous items, but not what she is searching for.

'What are you doing, woman?' cries Colin.

'Come and sit down immediately,' he demands, stabbing his finger at the empty chair.

'I had boxes and boxes of tablets, months of them stacked high, and now they've disappeared – whoosh! Like a puff of smoke. Where are they, Col?'

'For God's sake, Mother, give it a rest. I've moved them tidying up the cupboard. Here's your tablet box. It's where you left it.'

He waves it triumphantly like a flag.

Pat scoops up all of the assorted clutter on the work surface and slings it into the cupboard, slamming the doors shut, and lunges at Colin like a dog trying to grab a bone. Colin, wearing with pride his true colours, snatches his hand away and smirks.

The following evening, Pat is at the kitchen window again.

'That man is still at the gate. He's there most nights, just hanging around. He makes me shiver. There's something about him that I can't put my finger on. He must be bloody cold in this weather. He just wears those grey joggers with side stripes and his hoodie.'

'What man? Where?' enquires Colin, hiding in the pretence of his indifference, and, choking, sidles up to the window. He peeks over Pat's shoulder and, in his rudeness, coughs loudly, expelling spittle in her ear.

'There, there,' points Pat with her bent finger. 'He has lots of friends; they're always stopping to chat to him.'

The youth at the gate flashes his half-hidden eyes towards Pat's kitchen window and wanders off, disappearing into the dourness of the evening.

Pat notices a regular at the park waddle down the path with his overweight boxer by his side. They do say you get to be like your dog. *I used to look like my mutt, then I had to give him away*, reflects Pat. The man stops and waits for his squatting pet to relieve himself. Pat sighs as she notices the inconsiderate man has no doggie bags and makes no attempt to pick up the mess.

'Bloody people,' she mutters to herself.

Suddenly, she spots the youth at the gate again. He hops from one foot to the other with his hands deep in his pockets and she clocks him searching his surroundings. His shoulders are hunched with the weight of his intentions and, with an urgency, he glances back and forth, searching for prey like a hooded crow.

'That man's there again, Col,' Pat calls out.

'If I've told you once, I've told you a hundred times: put that bloody curtain down and let's have tea, and don't tell me it's beans on toast again.'

'Well, you know how things are, Col. We haven't got a penny to scratch our ass with.'

'I know, I know, it's not my fault. Thieving company stole my pension.' Colin grabs the tea towel and slings it across the room.

A few days pass much the same, when, suddenly, on Saturday evening, the front door swings open and there is Colin with a Lidl bag in hand, wearing a smile that's like an incoming tide splashing itself across his sand-coloured livery face.

'What's wrong with you?' asks Pat.

'Nothing, love, nothing,' beams Colin, 'but tonight we are going to eat in style. No more beans. I have two of the finest fillet steaks. Here, here.'

Clearing his throat, he takes them out of the bag and slams then down on the kitchen worktop, like a triumphant hunter displaying his kill. Pat takes one step backwards, unable to take her eyes off the plastic tray of meat, now bleeding in all its glory. Pat searches for words in the empty corridors of her mind.

'We can't afford these, for God's sake.'

'Yes, we can, but don't ask any more questions. It's my treat.'

Pat, drowning in the undertow of unknowing, silently fries the steaks. They sizzle laughingly in her face at her innocence, then spit their bloodied fat across the cracked tiles and spot her faded alopecia slippers. She takes some oven chips out of the cooker and places the spoils on the table. She winds herself once more onto a dining chair with a smile and emits a long-lost orgasmic sigh, as she lets her eyes stride across the banquet before her.

'Before we tuck in, I need my extra tablets. I can't find them anywhere,' she calls to Colin. 'I can't believe I'm running out. I had lots and now I don't seem to have hardly any. I need to take some with my food.'

'I don't know, Mother. Questions, questions. Now, just

shut up and eat your steak. It won't hurt you to miss them for once.'

They eat in consensual silence and sink their false teeth into the oozing steaks, biting and sucking at the flesh. Pat smiles with her Castrol lips at Colin, still lost in her blankness of thought.

Religiously, the following few evenings, Colin goes for a stroll, which is uncommon for him. Pat momentarily watches him saunter through the park and back again, and wonders if Colin should be going out with the cough he's had for the past few days.

Colin arrives once more through the front door and clears his throat.

'Made friends, have you, Col?'

'What do you mean, woman?'

'I've been watching you the last few evenings and you always stop to pass the time of day with that hoodie at the park gate.'

Colin freezes for a second, coughs loudly again, and busies himself around the kitchen, doing absolutely nothing.

The following evening, Colin disappears again.

Pat takes up her position, this time behind the protection of the nets. Suddenly, with a sharp intake of breath, she spots Colin handing a brown bag to the hoodie. The hoodie looks furtively around and passes Colin an envelope.

Old Mother Hubbard dives to the cupboard, searching again for her over-prescribed tablets, but alas the cupboard is bare.

PEACE AND JOY

Gold, frankincense and myrrh, precious gifts,
Moon mellow peeping from spidery web mist.
Silver bells call to the shining star,
Weary guests travelling from afar,
The argent beacon hauntingly brings.
Over frost-dipped hills in amity, carols ring.

Spellbound children search the skies,
Illusions of sleighs in their watchful eyes.
Nestling presents hug the tree,
Loving gifts to you from me.
Gleaming dust interspersed whips the pallid earth,
Virgin winged sweet angels sing, heralding Jesus' birth.

In the final hours of manic pace,
And the last till tings and lunacy fades.
Mother Nature, her pallid cloak slings,
Wrapping with love the last bird on the wing.
In twilight, her powdered sparkling beauty shines,
Flawless from rabid footprints, in passage of time.

Doily flakes flick grasslands dying blades,
And on the frozen fencing lays.
Gnarled ghostly limbs tap ashen keys,
With icy fingers on the breeze.
Peace, joy and solace amongst soothing trees,
Search your soul in silence, and in the stillness, BE.

PEACE OF MIND

Mind, cease your complex prevailing! thoughts,
emotions like flies in a web are caught.
Can't shake them off, held fast in suspension,
my head space aches with painful tension.

I have no control to make sedate,
when tears and fears collaborate.
I live my life without a reason,
that casts its stain upon each season.

Swirling, spinning, chaotic churning,
the fiery furnace of griefs keeps burning.
I wish the stars to sight the blind,
contentment is a peace of mind.

PEACE

In one transcendental moment,
A word can be captured, PEACE.
Amongst the sinews of our mind's hostilities.
We must always remind ourselves,
The value of love and compassion.
Be the PEACEmaker.
Surrender your cares,
Amongst battles the world has planned for you,
And quieten your war-weary senses.
Give yourself permission,
To nurture your inner being.
Find PEACE in the sacred light of your soul.
Retreat into your own space of silence.
Surrender your cares,
Amongst God's healing hands.
Give up the fight, invest in yourself.
Find PEACE in the perfect stillness,
And beauty of nature.
When journeying through the contagion,
of life's doom-laden darkest shadows,
Script your own happy ending,
And find your innermost PEACE.

PERSEID

From illuminating motes, my meteor man sprang,
To lighten this stargazer's chain of darkness.
My eyes looked upwards but remained dimmed,
Until my universe became you, and only you.
Indignations of frost, were lost,
In the sprinkling snow of hope,
From his unspoken words.
The dimension of my soul shone bright,
Then grew thin, with the sudden passing
Of the revelations of his sins.
The shimmering crystal ice,
Grew thicker within his brittle heart.
In pretence, I dusted over the cracks,
Of my mounting consternations.
I laid low beneath the luminous constellation.
The transference of my reflective love,
Shimmered high, but did not warm the night's sky.
I climbed, contemplative in my mind's eye,
to the outer reaches of the Heavens.
You fired your arrows bright,
Across the boughs of my passion.
With your coldness and insensitivity,
You snuffed me out.
Sanity was swiftly spent,

No longer to vent my emotions,
You showered me with permeating stars of kisses,
No flashing hits but swift the misses.
As quickly as you came, you left.
Bereft, I watched my meteor man,
Vanish into the shadows of the night.

HAIKU

PETALS

Petals float the streams,
Keeping their silken secrets,
And perfume the moon.

PANTOUM

POINTING TO NINE

There is no misery like the slow creeping of age in the unwinding of days.
Memories fade like the final tock of an echoing grandfather clock.
As the small ornate arthritic finger once again points to nine,
Forgetfulness devours my final hours in the clouding of my muddled mind.

Memories fade like the final tock of an echoing grandfather clock.
When minutes disappear within the creeping of death,
Forgetfulness devours my final hours in the clouding of my muddled mind,
And vacantly I stare into crannies of my room, searching for my redemption.

When minutes disappear within the creeping of death,
Wearily I stumble along the frosty paths of my lost youth,
And vacantly I stare into crannies of my room, searching for my redemption.
The bronzed pendulum swings like the sagging skin around my aching bones.

Wearily I stumble along the frosty paths of my lost youth.
There is no misery like the slow creeping of age in the unwinding of days,
The bronzed pendulum swings like the sagging skin around my aching bones,
As the small ornate arthritic finger once again points to nine.

HAIKU

POISONED FISH

Where poisoned fish lie.
The dress is not beautiful
When rivers are dyed.

PANTOUM

POPPY RED, POPPY RED

Shells scream, stabbing at the crimson skies as the evening crumbles.
A sickening stench of death fills the nostrils of men crying against the rain.
Alas, the poppies' flame rekindles a fading hope, as the echoes roll across the unyielding mantle of the earth.
The brave must not question the reasonings of war, which lay torn and threadbare at their feet.

A sickening stench of death fills the nostrils of men crying against the rain.
Bodies remain contorted in rivers of red, propped against the weeping banks of mud and slime.
The brave must not question the reasonings of war, which lay torn and threadbare at their feet.
Tirelessly, the devil hammers out his tune to the figures entombed with blood eyes.

Bodies remain contorted in rivers of red, propped against the weeping banks of mud and slime.
Gunshots of disbelief reverberate through unending twists and turns and cling to the shuddering of despair.

Tirelessly, the devil hammers out his tune to the figures entombed with blood eyes.

The red radiancy of glory grows dim, amongst the shallow blackness crawling on its belly in the corridors of Hell.

Gunshots of disbelief reverberate through unending twists and turns and cling to the shuddering of despair.

Shells scream, stabbing at the crimson skies as the evening crumbles.

The red radiancy of glory grows dim, amongst the shallow blackness crawling on its belly in the corridors of Hell.

Alas, the poppies' flame rekindles a fading hope, as the echoes roll across the unyielding mantle of the earth.

POTHOLES OF LIFE

'Bugger,' I growl under my breath as I attempt to avoid another pothole, but miss.

Ken's head rolls side to side. I give him a sideways glance and notice his eyelids drooping like heavy purses full of money. His wafer-thin skin, yellowy and aged, tells its own tale. Shadowy frets trace his face.

Ken's miraculous ringlets, alas, remain, bouncing like spring lambs across his furrowed forehead.

I hum in quietude to keep my spirits up whilst losing myself in the constituency of my thoughts. I hold onto the steering wheel in a vice-like grip. My ghostly white knuckles remain knotted at ten to two.

I swerve slightly as I try to avoid another pothole in the road, but alas it has the better of me. I cuss like a trooper once again, this time louder.

A black shiny motorbike passes, resembling the 1600cc cruiser we recently sold. How lovely it would have been to, once again, feel the wind in my hair. Ken, who spots it out of the corner of his eye, emits a heavy wistful sigh.

Trapped within his own isolation, his sleepy eyes then glance towards me.

'Going a little too fast, aren't we?' he sarcastically remarks.

I slow down slightly to appease him and throw him one of my frozen smiles. Lately, in our fifty-year marriage, I can't seem to do anything right, but it is understandable.

I remind myself of my vows all those years ago. In sickness and in health.

That was said with the naivety of youthful love.

I hit yet another pothole and the car shudders.

A grey BMW speeds past us, too close for comfort. Ken springs to life and gives him the finger. The placid man I once knew has turned to Mr Angry over many things.

The air remains toxic in the car. A cocktail of anger, fear, doubt and despair. It is up to me to remain jolly, but unfortunately it has become increasingly difficult. I try a distraction technique.

'Do you know Jean at number eight has finally got an appointment to have her hip replaced? Two years, she has been waiting – two years.'

Ken nods indifferently. *Probably not the right conversation at this moment in time*, I tell myself. Too depressing.

'The grandchildren are popping in tonight to see how things are. Bless them.'

I hum another tune but louder this time, so Ken can hear me. A shadow skips across the tearful sky as Ken shrinks into his own private dark space and ignores me.

The atmosphere in the car swallows us up as the stark grey building looms in the distance, beckoning us in.

I swing the car into the nearby car park and pull up into a spare parking space.

'Here we are again at our destination,' I say, a little too sharply and loudly.

I switch the engine off and wait to see if Ken makes the first move to clamber out.

After a short hesitation, he reaches across and places his hand on my knee and gives it a gentle squeeze.

In that briefest of moments, our tired eyes unite and the thinnest of smiles spread across our faces, uniting us once again in the love that often remains hidden but still exists.

'I don't really want to be here,' Ken shakily says.

'I know, I know,' I reply softly. 'But you have to fight; this is your only chance.'

I look tenderly at my one and only love once again.

As Ken steps gingerly out of the car, he catches his foot in a water-filled hole. I grab and steady him as he lets out a barrage of expletives.

'Come on, my darling, let's get you into the chemo room, and once again get this over with.'

Peeping through the clouds, a beam of sunshine finds its way into the foulness of the rippling puddled pothole and dances lightly upon the surface, bringing with it the tiniest ray of hope as we hold each other's hands.

HAIKU

REJECTION

On my knees I cried,
Crippled by rejection's blast.
I was cast aside.

SAFE IN THE SHALLOWS OF MY SOUL

Not too deep, I creep, amongst echoes,
Of my mind, where iridescent blue shoals,
Of past lugubrious lovers, swim by,
In thought-filled corridors of clouds.

Hung out to dry are haunting memories,
Of my rejected lovers' fading faces,
High on gallows, out of reach,
In the nebulous sky's gallery.

I attempt to study their features,
Which gradually dissipate,
Into the ether, of my own self-doubt,
Where the possibility of love was lost.

Menacing phantoms reappear,
To mock my insular life.
And in the dark veil of my world,
I lay justice to my lonely life.

In my ambitious mind,
I await with fever, a new coming.
My soulmate, my comforter,
Which I seek out in the storm clouds gathering.

In this tempest of my life, will you remain?
To kindle this frigid soul's flame.
Digging down deep,
I search out empathy.

Along with a defeated lost army of men,
I say farewell,
To my tranquil mind.
Alas, pretence throws me a lifeline.

I grasp onto the safety of the past.
And somersault backwards,
Back into the tentacles and tedium of time,
Where life was conformity and normality.

The slow pace of boredom kept me sane.
It was a time where I could swim on my back,
Look to the heavens and splash freely,
Without guilt weighing me down,
Safe in the shallows of my soul.

SCARLET SENTRY

Heaving heart with breast so red,
He's standing guard with slanted head.
Front and back with nervous twitch,
Stamping up and down his pitch.

Back and forth sharp eagle-eyed,
Spots intruders from the skies.
The sentry hops along his base,
Daring them to show their face.

All along the watchtower stands,
Showing them that he is grand.
Rifled wings, fine feathers bright,
He won't give up, without a fight.

Within his territory, food he guards,
Blocks of seeds and nuts and lard.
Chirruping, he dares them all,
The little soldier's marching tall.

Always first to greet the dawn,
On every frosty frigid morn.
He chirrups loud and, oh so sweet,
The echoes bounce along the street.

With sweetest face, and coat so grand,
I watch my Robin take his stand.

SEVERNSCAPE

A diminishing carmine drops dead weight,
upon the fuscous flowing channels of man's mystery.
An ebbing force sketches sweeping curvatures,
upon its coffee canvas.
A macramé of abandoned brushwood lies in defeat
cluttering the ever-changing contours of the scene.
Scrawled shadowy shapes appear,
and hug in their desperation the warps and wefts of rusty steel.
Lines support lines as solid and strong as one's own convictions.
Beneath the girders, secret sable abstractions,
quiver in the shipwreck of trapped time.
Leaded peace, saying nothing and going nowhere,
wraps itself around the briny wrinkles of the Severn's veins.
Transmitted tear-stained rays kiss each blackened frown,
and soothes in silence the deep dark waters.
A pier in one long stride, spreads itself outwards,
calling to its familiar shores with a quiet voice.
In the confusion of dishevelled tides,
brush strokes of forgotten blistered vegetation,
highlight sparse sections of cloth.

Am I imposing on a masterpiece,
stumbling across the many rocky pebbles of life?
Coupled with the occasional screeching scavenger,
scanning for outcasts pulsating in puddles,
I tread stealthily, so not to crowd the canvas,
allowing the breeze to blow gently on my dusty heart.
Such artistry. Can I but paint within you reflected images?
Created coastline. A painting named "Severnscape".

The artist is GOD.

PANTOUM

SINNER ON THE SOUTHERN LINE

An unholy figure amongst the throng sways like a bough in the breeze, drooping with heavy fruit.
The killer grips the train's leather strap and stares ahead with an absence locked in her dark eyes.
In a blank state, she senses the staleness of her surroundings as the flow of aborted life tickles the inside of her legs.
Hiding the falseness of the truth, she swallowed the sinful pills, leaving her torment to travel along the never-ending steel tracks of time.

The killer grips the train's leather strap and stares ahead with an absence locked in her dark eyes.
The language of pain is written in the deep frets smirching the woman's brow.
Hiding the falseness of truth, she swallowed the sinful pills, leaving her torment to travel along the never-ending steel tracks of time.
Didactic religion in all of its tarnished glory tossed away her dreams in a moment of madness.

The language of pain is written in the deep frets appearing on the woman's brow.
Travelling South, underground, wrapped in the stale blanket of false beliefs, she feels the stabbing pain.
Didactic religion in all of its tarnished glory tossed away her dreams in a moment of madness.
Bereft, she followed her faith that lay locked and frozen in time, and is pitiful in its corruption.

Travelling South, underground, wrapped in the stale blanket of false beliefs, she feels a stabbing pain.
An unholy figure amongst the throng sways like a bough in the breeze, drooping with forbidden fruit.
Bereft, she followed her faith that lay locked and frozen in time, and is pitiful in its corruption.
In a blank state, she senses the staleness of her surroundings as the flow of aborted life tickles the inside of her legs.

SLEEP APNOEA

Bert snatches at his plastic trunk and flings it sideways.

'I tell you, Mabel, I'm fed up with this contraption. Fed up, I tell you, fed up.'

'Well, it's wearing that or I'm sure I shall murder you in your sleep,' Mabel wearily replies.

'Charming, I must say. Last night, I woke up with my upper lip numb as an idler's bum. I had to feel where it was with my fingers. The damn contraption had shifted in the night and the elastic had cut off the blood supply to my upper lip,' snaps Bert.

'Well, it seems to be working alright now,' whispers Mabel.

'What did you say, Mabel? What did you say?'

'Nothing, dear, nothing.'

'No, they don't tell you about numb lips in the instructions. No. You have to find that out for yourself,' witters Bert. 'Look, I'm getting up to make a cuppa, do you want one?'

'OK, OK, anything that makes you happy.'

Mabel, feeling shaky, sighs with the sheer relief of his absence and yanks the duvet over to her side of the bed, making sure she has the lion's share before Bert reappears.

A few minutes later, Bert waddles back to their bedroom with a tray of tea and swallows up the door frame like a huge cumulus cloud in his polyester pyjamas. A loosely tied cord searches hopelessly for the disappearing waistline.

'And also,' he booms, 'nobody told me about the humidifier having to be in the bedroom to stop me having a runny nose.' He sniffs loudly to prove his point.

Bert, wheezing slightly, places the tray of slopping tea on the bedside table and heaves himself once more onto the bed.

'It's alright for you, laying still on your side. I can only lie flat on my back, like a filleted turbot on a fishmonger's slab. I know I need that stupid gas mask on to help me breathe, but you prodding me in the ribs every few seconds when I don't doesn't contribute to a good night's sleep either. No wonder I am always tired. I'm sure you are the cause of my sleeplessness, not my apnoea. And another thing. No, I'm not fat. I'm just portly like most men of my age. Anyway, my physique has certainly turned you on a few times in the past. Maybe not now, I grant you, but you're always weary anyway. You should visit the doctor and get some sleeping tablets instead of blaming me for your tiredness, and you should stop wittering on about sleeping in different beds. I've always slept with you, Mabel, and I don't intend to change now. Anyway, separate beds are the first signs of deterioration in a marriage. Are you listening, Mabel?'

Bert, tweaking his dewlap, glances angrily at Mabel. He cannot believe his eyes. Mabel is sound asleep.

He prods her sharply in the ribs, but to no avail.

'Mabel, Mabel!' he screams, but thankfully she cannot hear him in her deep sleep.

PANTOUM

SNOWDROP

A chaste snowdrop waves her frills of truce,
Amongst the grim harshness of the earth.
Displaying hope for mankind in the peace of the day,
The fragile flower blooms sweetly in defiance.

Amongst the grim harshness of the earth,
Midwinter plays its nefarious games.
The fragile flower blooms sweetly in defiance,
Amongst brittle limbs and befuddled snow-coated cobwebs.

Midwinter plays its nefarious games,
Upon the deathly dormant calcifying pages of fields.
Amongst brittle limbs and befuddled snow-coated cobwebs,
Soft, saintly angel feathers fall in heavenly quietude.

Upon the deathly dormant calcifying pages of fields,
A chaste snowdrop waves her frills of truce.
Soft, saintly angel feathers fall in heavenly quietude,
Displaying hope for mankind in the peace of the day.

SNOWFLAKES

Blowing the mantle of the earth,
With a chilling breath,
Flicking winter's chilled grave,
Where deep the saintly sleep,
Snowflakes lay a dusting of death,
Where the phantoms footprints creep.

Heavy as a sinner on the gallows,
A quietus of snow and frost,
Crowns the tombs of the silent night,
And frozen kisses, tossed, take flight.
A church bell rides the backs of echoes,
Wrapping the bare bones of boughs in a comfort fleece.

Snowflakes flutter in the rejoicing,
Of their freedom,
And surrender upon the hoary-headed frost,
Leaving a sprinkling of dust upon the earth.
Ashen-faced ghosts rise from tombs,
And float in their clouds of restlessness.

Dancing down from the Heavens,
Snowflakes rejoice in the purity they place upon our world.
A moment of great calm fills the vast emptiness,
And lies in wait in the silence of the shadows.
Snowflakes encapsulate my fragile mind,
With awe, and wonder, and purge my aching soul.

SOCIETY

Incalculable rage,
Permeates through our society.
Mass migration,
Foreigners arriving by boats,
Put before our own.
No room at the inn.
Lost family connections
Substituted with serried groups,
Aimlessly waving banners and flags.
Wear a badge, belong,
With no perceived knowledge,
Of their protestations.
Above the face coverings,
Basilisk stares.
Eyes of darkness peering out,
Are conditioned to hate,
By certain religious groups.
Many programmed academia
Also follow the flock like sheep,
And chant vociferously,
About issues they know nothing about.
Mosques spring up,
In defiance of our religion.
Christian crosses crumble in apathy,

Along with the congregation.
Left, far right,
Who cares?
Anarchy is in the air.
Nonconformists,
Become scapegoats.
Silence the dissenters,
The freedom of speech,
Has become obsolete.
Nothing controversial,
Must be heard.
Must we all acquiesce?
Evil minds celebrate,
At the gates of prisons,
With champagne.
The release of rapists,
Make way in prisons,
for the majority,
Of sensible people,
Releasing tensions,
From their forbearance, online.
Indefatigable rants from politicians,
Erode our minds.
Culture is a dirty word,

Monuments must be destroyed.
Our streets have been given over,
To keep the peace,
Controlled by two-tier policing.
To appease foreign prejudices.
With the primacy of government,
With self-inflicted Sisyphean tasks,
The aged are seen as a blight on society,
A burden with their disobedient votes.
Paid into the system, but steal their coffers,
Leave behind empty pots of promises.
Veterans exigences ignored,
Second-class citizens,
Now in turbid surroundings.
Sleeping in tents or on streets.
Yet they gave their lives for our freedom.
I am not biased,
With my opinions,
Neither am I prejudiced.
In this crazy world.
I am honest to say,
I distrust all people,
Equally, especially politicians!

THE SURFER

Spiting energetic seas,
Effervescence swirls my knees.
Surf with screeching granite gulls,
soaring to the breeze.
Roll over, rays of light in tunnel,
Funnel to my death?
Swallowed in a silvery smile,
Sucked into briny breath.
Frothing foam, tossing me,
Through crazed cascading seas.
Balanced on your raging back,
Feeling wild and free.
Race me on my fibre frame,
To beach in manic gush,
Bobbing like buoy 'tween the waves,
Raise me up in adrenalin rush.

SWEET SUSAN

Fred steps backwards to admire his rose, 'Sweet Susan' – the one he's entering in the local flower show. Ironically, it has the same name as his wife, minus the sweet. He uncurls his stiffening spine and places a stained palm on his hip. Fred huffs with guilt in the conspiracy of the silence. The peace is littered with memories of the argument he and his wife had a week prior.

The satanic buds have begun to blossom. He mixes his bone meal again with the darkened blood and trowels it deeply around the tubers, and waters Susan with the falseness of his tears.

PANTOUM

THE ASPIRATIONS OF ANGELS

I stroll amongst the brooding darkness, mantled by a mystical mist.
Upon the ethereal skies, my approaching end is scripted.
As my epitaph is scrawled in fairy dust amongst the sinking of the day,
The moon slowly rises above the Severn and shines its magical light.

Upon the ethereal skies, my approaching end is scripted.
This life's fairy-tale, has it a happy ending?
The moon slowly rises above the Severn and shines its magical light,
As I stumble along the ragged shores of my disappearing world.

This life's fairy tale, has it a happy ending?
Did I achieve the aspirations of angels?
As I stumble along the ragged shores of my disappearing world,
I feel the soft breeze on my cheek kissing me goodbye.

Did I achieve the aspirations of angels?
I stroll amongst the brooding darkness, mantled by a mystical mist.
I feel the soft breeze on my cheek kissing me goodbye,
As my epitaph is scrawled in fairy dust, amongst the sinking of the day.

THE BIRD FEEDER

Under his Perspex helmet, the hawkish Home Guard peers.
A Luftwaffe rolls his hips and lobs him a bomb of splattered tears.
With pin-prick seedy, beady eyes and toothless mouth agape,
Dampened by the last sweetness of the clouds, the feeder waits.

Tides of tiny bright blue tits, like hectic spots and spits,
Splash with greed the grainy rain, scattering the grit.
Dagger-beaked carrion crows with grins of impiety,
Gloss with murderous laughter the grumblings of the sky.

The Home Guard flicks his pick and mix from hardened gums and sways.
With stiff upper lip, the unlit beacon beckons the hungry of the day.
Undeterred, an enemy stalks in his quest to squirrel for grist.
The victor lunges at the hood, raising in triumph seed in his fist.

The Home Guard bows in disbelief at rusty shells beneath his feet,
The zero mouth that cannot speak is lost for words, blanked in defeat.

THE BRIEFEST OF SECONDS

He presses the buzzer again and again, but nobody comes. He presses it once more. He waits in anticipation for a nurse to come and help him. Hope is all he clings to. Hope is the ticking clock in life that keeps us sane through the devouring of age. He silently mouths a conversation to himself as the monotonous seconds tick by. The old man wipes the drip from his aquiline nose in the sleeve of his institutionalised pyjamas.

Tamir sighs and leans back into the comfort of his pillow. He digs deep into the savagery of the years that surrounded his childhood and turns over the sods of undying grief, like he has time and time again.

How his life has turned full circle. Here he is again in striped pyjamas and kippah. Once more, he feels the deep emotions of helplessness and loneliness bubble to the surface. Sobering thoughts he had attempted to bury from his youth, when the world was coloured with ills, have appeared again, pricking his conscience, and lay themselves like thorns around his bed. Why was he the only one in his family to survive?

Tamir glances at the muted screen glaring down from the stark wall and stares blankly at the scene of rubble and the burnt-out embers of a city in the far east. Ah, he tells himself, with the stillness of his tongue. Nothing changes; life goes on; wars continue. Wars where everyone loses, nobody wins and only one language is spoken – the language of Hell.

Tamir licks his chapped lips and prays for a drink. The pain in his abdomen still remains, but, as he told himself, not as much pain as the ache that permanently remains in his heart. His memories take him back to his family, his mother, father and sisters. Faces of the past, faded and lost in the passage of time.

He suddenly catches sight of an effervescent girl pushing a trolley. 'Hello, darling,' she chirrups with all the naivety of youth. 'Would you like a cuppa? It's good old Yorkshire.'

'Please,' Tamir whispers, 'I'm parched – and maybe, if I'm not a nuisance, some painkillers.'

He studies her waves of burnt red hair swept on top of her head like a stook and held together with a scrunchy. A few tongues of flames have escaped and cascade down her face, kissing her pale moon cheeks. Her soft blue eyes, full of ignorance, stare quizzically at Tamir.

'Any sugar, love?'

'No, thanks,' he wearily replies.

As Tamir stretches out his scrawny arm, his pyjama sleeve slides up.

Rosie notices a faded tattoo on his arm. *Why would anyone want numbers on their flesh?* she ponders. *It's not as good as my Chinese dragon on my back.*

The old man shakily takes the cup of tea.

'Toda.'

'Sorry,' Rosie replies.

'Thank you, dear,' Tamir whispers.

He reminds himself that although people say that the National Health Service is in crisis, he is eternally grateful to graze – with his crumbling of strength – on the pastures of this green and pleasant land. He came and found his Jerusalem amongst the dark satanic mills many years ago when he lived up to his name 'tall, upright'.

Rosie feels a little compassion for the old gentleman in the hospital bed. He reminds her of her grandfather, who had died a year ago. She stretches out her hand and gently squeezes his. A tear finds its way onto his cheek, which takes him by surprise. A tear he vowed with stoic pride he would never show this crazy, brutal world.

They hold hands for the briefest of time and glance at each other. She, with the blindness of her innocence; he, with his half-closed eyes, trying desperately to focus on her face. Time stands still for the briefest of seconds as they bridge the gap between east and west.

THE BRUTAL SHORES OF MY WORLD

The shadowy ghosts of my former self stretch out from my feet,
Like tides of flat floundering dabs, along the cold solitary beach.
The grainy air swallows up the inaudible cursing of my misery.
The sap of suffering corkscrews me into the curvaceous dunes.
My grunts and groans bubble and foam in the rip-rap of hurt,
Surfing my ulcered mouth like a salient sweet.
Memories stain my mind with their oil-polluting piercing ink.
How I wish to draw the lines of my life in the sand.
Re-enactments of events remain in the currents of my spiralling drop.
Ocean masters race up my spine, pricking the corners of my consciousness.
Swirling and shunted in the tide's brainstorm of pain,
Like the driftwood's face pushed into the sand,
I spit out the grains of sadness and crawl towards the sea.
The battle of breathing in the tempest becomes a chore.
No rescuing ethereal hand in the stinging shards of rain.
My eyes hurt seeing the vacancy of the blackened flow of the sea.
I rise and fall like the determined waves screaming out to the breaking of the day,
As I smash myself to pieces along the brittle shores of my drowning world.

ANTOUM

THE CIMMERIANS

We meet in the gloom, mantled by death's mist, where life's light is fading fast.
The brooding darkness of the night arrives and takes its deathly bite,
Whilst the nomads and I walk together in dreams alongside the Black Sea,
An unkind raven's wing falls to blanket out my lonely night.

The brooding darkness of the night arrives and takes its deathly bite.
Along the ragged edge of the world, Hades hears my call.
An unkind raven's wing falls to blanket out my lonely night.
This moribund, a shadow of my former self, searches for a rendering of the soul.

Along the ragged edge of the world, Hades hears my call.
In my mind's perpetual darkness, the Cimmerians enter.
This moribund, a shadow of my former self, searches for a rendering of the soul.
I await in the luminous darkness for the script of my unhappy ending.

In my mind's perpetual darkness, the Cimmerians enter.
We meet in the gloom, mantled by death's mist, where life's light is fading fast.
I await in the luminous darkness for the script of my unhappy ending,
Whilst the nomads and I walk together in dreams alongside the Black Sea.

PANTOUM

THE COTSWOLDS

A raptor with dark intentions circles the blue axle of Heaven, and dives upon the Cotswolds.
The morning rays thatch the verdant blades and wildflowers that run nowhere in particular.
As a soft-speaking breeze nets my breath and blows its gentle kisses on my wanton lips.
I climb up, not back, through sunshine rapeseed, which purges my mind with tranquillity.

The morning rays thatch the verdant blades and wildflowers that run nowhere in particular.
Comforting homes of buttered stone lay strewn amongst the undulations of my world.
I climb up, not back, through sunshine rapeseed, which purges my mind with tranquillity.
Life's dawn ignites the earth's mantle and places her healing hand upon my fretful brow.

Comforting homes of buttered stone lay strewn amongst the undulations of my world.
An echo of a birthing cow runs amok through the silence of the hills and takes possession.
Life's dawn ignites the earth's mantle and places her healing hand upon my fretful brow.
Churches weep with unanswered questions nailed on crosses, memorials to vanishing faces.

An echo of a birthing cow runs amok through the silence of the hills and takes possession.
A raptor with dark intentions circles the blue axle of Heaven, and dives upon the Cotswolds.
Churches weep with unanswered questions nailed on crosses, memorials to vanishing faces.
As a soft-speaking breeze nets my breath and blows its gentle kisses on my wanton lips.

PANTOUM

THE COVID-19 SHEEP

Once again, loneliness yawns in time's violent torrent,
With repeated orders of self-isolation, we reluctantly obey.
My brass clock strikes three and jeers at the hopelessness of the future.
Virtue signalling with nappies, in the damp day, sheep's bleats are trapped.

With repeated orders of self-isolation, we reluctantly obey.
Behind the scenes, a vaccine is in the making. Hell is empty, the devils are here.
Virtue signalling with nappies, in the damp day, sheep's bleats are trapped.
Are flocks unaware of the sustained misery bestowed when permanently fenced in?

Behind the scenes, a vaccine is in the making. Hell is empty, the devils are here.
Herded sheep obey within their troughs of ignorance, the bellwether beasts, the government.
Are flocks unaware of the sustained misery bestowed when permanently fenced in?
Poisoned sheep trot by my home, two metres apart, defeatism locked and frozen in their eyes.

Herded sheep obey within their troughs of ignorance, the bellwether beasts, the government.
Once again, loneliness yawns in time's violent torrent.
Poisoned sheep trot by my home, two metres apart, defeatism locked and frozen in their eyes.
My brass clock strikes three and jeers at the hopelessness of the future.

PANTOUM

THE CREEPING OF YOUR CANCER

I wander lonely with my thoughts through pillars of the night.
Words of love I must strew, in early morning's light.
Along vast halls of darkness, I kiss your pallid face.
As time together ebbs away, sobs fill my empty space.

Words of love I must strew, in early morning's light.
Sometimes creeping cancer blinds my very sight.
As time together ebbs away, sobs fill my empty space.
Whilst deathly figures mock my doubt, keeping up their pace.

Sometimes creeping cancer blinds my very sight.
A frost of woes hang heavy and fills my heart with fright.
Whilst deathly figures mock my doubt, keeping up their pace,
I gently search new tumours, and with my fingers trace.

A frost of woes hang heavy and fills my heart with fright.
I wander lonely with my thoughts, through pillars of the night.
I gently search new tumours, and with my fingers trace.
Along vast halls of darkness, I kiss your pallid face.

HAIKU

THE DARK SOUL

He, with a dark soul,
Feels the winter of despair,
Locked in his own cell.

PANTOUM THAT CAN BE READ IN REVERSE

THE DEAD MOCK IN THEIR PEACE

With sharp nailed hooves, time creeps,
Through woes that blind our sight,
The dead mock in their peace,
Between life's frets, that bite.

Through woes that blind our sight,
Into ourselves, we leap,
Between life's frets, that bite,
Bereft, we search for sleep.

Into ourselves, we leap,
Breathless for hope's light,
Bereft, we search for sleep,
In the conspiracies of night.

Breathless for hope's light,
With sharp nailed hooves, time creeps.
In the conspiracies of night,
The dead mock in their peace.

THE DUTY VISIT

The starlings cloak the sombre skies, dropping, coiling, towering, dive,
Amongst their dance, my weekly appeasement, your car arrives.
Scarred past, too needy, my love's a smothering blanket, too sickly sweet,
With a downwards glance, you say, "Hi." I must not be greedy, your eyes and mine don't meet.

Struggling, I catch inane words in a net, muttering grouch about the weather,
I say, "I'm fine." You say the same. Keep it light and as soft as a feather.
I play boring, no questions, nothing too deep,
Your shallow mother in a darkened cupboard you keep.

Numbed, I make a cup of tea and offer you cake. You bite a little and say,
Your family is waiting, time is too precious and you can't really stay.
You look tired, crippled, weary, my son, I can tell by your eyes,
Your burden is far too weighty; your path too lengthy and wide.

I try to grasp the moment, before you disappear,
An aching sadness engulfs me. My mind is full of fear.
I want to talk deeply but you say, "Mum, goodbye."
You've said many times, "Don't go there, don't even try."

My middle-aged son, I kiss your neck as you turn away,
It is not a weakness to give me a hug. I wish you could stay.
My empty heart aches, I wave at your car, crushing tears I force back,
The starlings, searching for home, curl, soar, dip and cry, and the skies turn satanic black.

FOOT AND MOUTH

Deep as furrowed land, the beaten brow shielded by hand,
Concealing face that braved the storm, but now is beaten so forlorn.
He tries to hide the briny tears, that shows the wrenching pain that sears,
Flat-capped warrior sobbing sighs, and feels the shame, when broken cries.
His hands are tied, what can he do, the gunman seeks the trembling ewe.
And in God's green and pleasant land, sinister men arrive in bloodstained vans.
Snap, snap, the guns echo on high, screeching crows circle sullen sky.
Smoking clouds of putrefied pyres, stoked by Satan, rises higher.
Clenched fists, so wrung that toiled so hard, corpses strewn on farmer's yards.
Brain so fogged the farmer's beaten, breakfast plates with food half eaten.
Does he try to pick up the pieces of his life amongst death, blood and faeces?
Has he got strength to start again, or are his efforts all in vain?
With shoulders slumped in threadbare chair, he picks up his gun to his grey temple hair.

And who really cares?

THE FINALTY OF OUR WORLD

What is taking place with our climate,
Whilst we are awake or asleep?
What conspirators are
Chalking paths with vapour trails?
Who are playing games,
With global temperatures,
And filling skies with dire consequences,
That scratch the vacancy of space?
What is the validity of their experiments,
Using silver or potassium iodine, or dry ice?
Tomorrow yet again, the rain sobs upon us sheep,
Depressing and suppressing the joyousness of life.
Our hopes dissipate into nothingness.
We have become desensitised,
So, we cannot think for ourselves,
About the consequences of the powerful,
Playing with nature,
For their own greedy monetary rewards.
Plasticity; will we be able,
To restructure our brains,
In the light of our experiences,
And understand the dangerous games?
With global temperatures astray,
Will we destroy our planet?

Ambiguous are my thoughts,
That torture this verse.
My temples pulsate with unanswered questions.
Planes of poison circle overhead.
Will future geoengineering technology add,
To the deficiencies of the present day?
Maybe only this insomniac,
Tunes into the secret germination,
Of the government's darkest plans.
Whilst the country lays dormant at night,
Or zombie-like awake, in sombre days,
The colours of our world are slowly dying.
From the unforeseen damnation,
Open our fettered eyes to the truth,
Of the cloud seeding taking place.
Let us awaken, and be aware
Of the corruption, and contamination,
Taking place, by the powers that be,
To control temperatures,
Before it is too late.
We must ask the question,
Who is playing God,
As the darkness gathers?

THE FIRE OF FATE

'Want more bloody food, do you?' snaps Malcolm, as he rams a log sideways into the smouldering hungry mouth of the open fire. The log crackles loudly as the heap of grey ash below collapses. He shuffles over to the window and pulls the curtains tightly together, blanking out the closing lids of the day and the slow creep, creeping of the endless night.

'Thank God, another day over,' he mutters to himself. Malcolm catches sight of the photograph of his beautiful smiling wife in a silver frame on the mantlepiece. Her dark brown eyes seem to follow him as he crosses the room to study her more closely. He emits a wandering sigh. The grandfather clock in the hall stabs at the silence and, after a loud clunk, slowly strikes five. One, two, three, four, five.

Jean was a good wife, he ponders. *Always got my tea on time and kept a clean house. I didn't want her to work; her duty was to see to the house and, first and foremost, me.* Malcolm shivers slightly and hugs his holey cardigan, with missing buttons, closely to his chest.

'How I miss you, Jean. Why did you have to go? I could do with you now. You were always good at darning and sewing the buttons on my clothes, and now the blasted things are always falling off just to annoy me,' he mutters angrily to himself through the steely bars of his teeth.

'Well, what shall I have for tea tonight?' he calls to his absent wife through his broth of spittle. 'I suppose it will have to be beans on toast again.'

He wipes his cracked mouth on the frayed cuff of his cardigan. Malcolm had never learnt to cook, but why did he need to? After all, he stubbornly tells himself in his shallow blankness, he had his Jean.

He remembered all those years ago when his obedient wife, Jean, had faithfully tended to his every need. She was the perfect wife and, in his unspoken words, he had loved her for that. Malcolm remembers Jean longing for children, but they could not afford them – after all, his job as postman couldn't feed more than two mouths, he repeatedly told her, refusing to let his reasoning turn amongst her pitiful begging.

He repeats his unanswered questions again and again. 'Why did you have to go? We were perfect together.'

Malcolm shuffles into the kitchen and prises open a small can of beans. Fifty per cent less sugar, he notices on the label. Not that it means a jot to him, as he had always been tall and lean. It must have been all the walking he had to do with his job. Malcolm notices the food stains from previous angers clinging to the damp walls near the kitchen door – the one with the smashed panel. The miscreant lifts his thoughts from a depth too morose for tears that he does not want to revisit and blindly fixes his eyes on the job in hand, to get his own tea.

He burns the toast but doesn't care. He viciously scrapes it with a knife over the sink and spreads the Anchor butter over the burnt toast like a brickie with wet cement, finishing with a layer of baked beans that had previously stuck like shit to a shovel in the saucepan.

Malcolm carefully carries his plate, knife and fork into the lounge and slumps once again into his favourite chair by the fireside, casting his mind back to his childhood. All his childhood memories are mantled by the inherent mist of unhappiness and a fear not spoken about. Malcolm, stuffing his face, recalls his father, who would sit by the fire like him with a constant frown of regret on his brow. His father would hold within his crude hands a large plate of bread and dripping, and place it firmly on his lap. He would stab the bread onto a fork and hold it over the licking flames of the fire. Malcolm and his siblings were never allowed any and would watch, licking their lips in silence as their father, who was head of the family and the breadwinner, stuffed the contents of his meal into the ugly greasy scar of his mouth. Hunger in all of its forms uncurled itself within their home. At least toasting bread made light work for the harshness of his father's hands.

Malcolm, finishing his meal with relish, recalls his mother – a slip of a thing who did not speak much. She was always ailing and scuttled into the corners of their house like a frightened mouse. She never smiled – *a bit like Jean in the last years we were together*, he ponders. Malcolm never knew what was wrong with his timid mother, only that she was clumsy, always bumping into things and covered in bruises. Jean bruised easily, he tells himself absent-mindedly. Malcolm finds his memories are travelling towards the direction of reality, so changes tack, fearfully not wanting to awaken the truth.

Malcolm clears his throat and casts his eyes once more towards his wife's photograph. *She is happy there*, he tells himself, *so it wasn't all bad.*

She was always contented when they first married, but then, over time, he noticed a change in her, and in the last few years together he could not bring to mind her smiling face. Jean was a bubbly person, but slowly her effervescence became flat like a long-opened bottle of her favourite La Gioiosa sparkling prosecco. Jean had secretly tried it once in a neighbour's house and fallen in love with it. She was never allowed to buy prosecco because Malcolm thought it was a waste of money and it only made her mellow, which would cause a ripple of tears to fall down her sunken cheeks. Malcolm made sure her pleasures were not allowed in the house. A darkness fell upon her drained face, which washed out the colours of her life. She finally became a shadow of her former self.

Malcolm stares fixedly at the fire, trying to rob it of its heat. He stubbornly refuses to feel the cold wind of truth blowing silently around his feet. When had she let him out of her life and let herself in?

Malcolm's mind hopscotches between the memories of his childhood and his marriage. He was like a taut string of a bow, stretched between the past and future. Now father and wife were both gone – the latter he missed dreadfully – and all Malcolm could do now was sit alone in the sour shadows of his room, wretched in his mutterings.

The police broke down the door to Malcolm's house two weeks later as Ahmed from the corner shop, who put

Malcolm's *Daily Mail* newspapers aside for him, reported that he had not been in for a while, and also neighbours had said his curtains had not been pulled.

The police forced their way into Malcolm's house and called out from the hall, before finally bursting through the faded magnolia door of his lounge. He was nowhere to be seen. One policeman strode over to the window and pulled back the lounge curtains to let more daylight in, which smashed against the shores of the room's darkness. The dull light, which held a strangeness all of its own, filled the room. The fire in the grate had long been extinguished and all that remained were ashes. Alongside the grate was the armchair, also blanketed with a mound of grey dust. Two human limbs pocking out from scorched grey trouser legs and wearing faded green slippers on their feet remained intact and spreadeagled amongst some of the cursed scatterings that had spilled precariously from the armchair over the multicoloured Axminster carpet.

A silence descended upon the room as the three burly policemen with their eyes firmly fixed on the scene before them tried to absorb what they were witnessing.

'Christ, we have an SHC here,' shouted the elder of the three.

'What?' replied the youngest.

'Spontaneous human combustion,' answered the most knowledgeable policeman.

With the policemen's heavy breathing, coughing and spluttering amongst the stale air, their eyes darted around the lounge and finally became focused. They found their resting place upon the photograph of Malcolm's wife with an enigmatic smile staring at them from a silver frame. The daylight danced upon her haunting face, which now held its own peculiar peace.

They also noticed a faded postcard on the carpet near the burnt legs. A young pale-faced policeman stooped low and carefully retrieved it. He noticed by the postmark that it had been sent from Bournemouth a few years ago and was signed by Jean. The words in bold letters read, 'BURN IN HELL'.

Alas, her wishes were granted!

THE FROG

Squashed like a tongue between clenched teeth,
Bubble-eyed I stare, seeing nothing, but taking in everything.

The snaking embrocating mist lubricates my camouflaged spine,
With the fondling of its smooth cold fingers.

I squat amongst the swaddling reeds,
As a dank blanket cloaks the wetlands with a chill.

Croaks in unison echo across the calling site.
We wait, in anticipation, of a fleeting kamikaze fly.

The odd disturbed bird sketches circles with its pinions,
Whilst calling to the oncoming darkness with dulcet tones,

The hour comes in late, and in the mocking of the mist,
Nature with its changing behaviour sweeps the tide inside out.

I stare vacantly into the feculent water and strange light,
Reflecting my past in the awaiting of my future.

Staring, staring once again from the banks,
Into the dull, deep mirrors of my soul.

HAIKU

THE FUNNELLED HOLE

*In the funnelled hole,
A fidgeting mouse peeps out,
And loses its head!*

THE GHOSTLY TUNE

Dawn's morning breath picks itself up and leaves like flaming claws scratch the sombre stonework of the church as the clock strikes six. A weary lone figure crunches through the ochre confetti pushing a pram. Dusty fragments of her marriage vows blow like the autumn's breath around her dizzy head. She knew from the crumbs fed to her by her so-called friends that he always crossed the churchyard on his way back from the seedy club he frequented at the weekends. He never left the club until all the housekeeping and rent money was spent.

Violet's baby had woken in the early hours and had become fractious. Even holding him to her breast did not satisfy his want. He was unsettled and would not feed, so she decided to take him for a walk, which always had the desired effect to make him sleep. It was also an excuse not to crawl back, once again, into her empty bed.

Violet sees her husband's silhouette in the swirling mist and recognises his cocky swagger. He saunters through the church gate in his grey pinstriped suit, with his smart jacket wide open and his hands sunk deep into his now-empty trouser pockets. He whistles a staccato tune, which is so unbecoming on a holy day. How she had loved that dusky figure in his slanted fedora but so had many other women. She slams on the brakes of the black Silver Cross pram and hovers by the cold, unforgiving church steps. For a moment, he looks curiously surprised to see her, but that soon fades as he begins to curse her. A smirk slowly appears under his dark moustache as he announces he doesn't love her anymore and never really had, due to her always stalking him, which is totally unfounded. However, he likes to watch her wounds open and bleed.

In the stillness, dawn's truth awakens, and an uncontrollable stirring of hate rises deep from within Violet's inner self. It totally consumes her frailness and finally bursts forth with the sickening vengeance of a woman scorned. Becoming stronger in her weakness, she knows that if she can't have him, no one can.

In an instant, Violet pulls out a large brass pin from the green velvet hat perched on the back of her head and stabs it as hard as her strength can muster through his waistcoat, narrowly missing his Albert chain, and right into his frozen heart.

A look of shock suddenly eats up his face and, tottering unsteadily on his feet, he falls backwards, smacking his head upon the concrete step with a thud. His black fedora escapes in terror across the dank pathway and into the harvest of the tarnished grass. Nobody should be seen on the Sabbath without their hat on, Violet reminds herself, as she picks it up and flings it across his handsome, startled face.

The hungry baby begins to wail uncontrollably in the hostile air. Violet carefully wipes her hat pin with a handkerchief – still sweetly smelling of 'An Evening in Paris' and embroidered with the letter 'J' – she'd found in her husband's coat pocket, and pushes it, with a strong determination, back into her hat.

The early morning mist swirls menacingly around mother and baby as they vanish like inhabitants from another world into the cold, thin, wispy air, never to be seen again.

Every year on the same day, as the church clock strikes six, a cock crows three times and a ghostly whistling tune can be heard resonating throughout the churchyard. Upon a cold, cracked, mouldy gravestone, a thorny red rose is placed to perish upon a sinner's bones.

THE GIFT OF LOVE

Hilary stooped to pick up her sparkling diamanté dance shoes and sighed. The hours of the week had once again dragged their feet through the silent tracks of time, but at last Saturday's salsa class had arrived. Although the class consisted of oceans of widows, Saturday was the only day that bought a little light relief from the yawning loneliness Hilary had experienced over the last six months. An emptiness had nailed itself to the walls of her home and she had sealed herself inwards, attempting to hide from the pain of grief lingering bare-headed in the shadows of the cold winter nights. Her husband of fifty years had slowly died from cancer, which had begun in the prostate and eventually travelled to all of his bones. She nursed him but watched helplessly as death shook hands with life. Her husband tried many different treatments, but to no avail, and began withering away like an unwatered flower.

Many emotions headed by raging anger busied themselves in Hilary's head until she was too exhausted to weep and, realising her grief was too deep for tears, she gradually gave up on herself. *What was the point of trying to keep up appearances?* she asked herself. Wisps of grey strands were crawling through her chestnut-brown dyed hair and her make-up was now non-existent. Robotically, she struggled through each brutal day, seeing only lonely footprints leading to herself. Her brief chat in the morning with Eric, who served her with newspapers and milk from the corner shop, was only one of the few contacts with the outside world she had. He always made polite conversation, but that was it. Little did she know that he, too, had walked in her shoes five years previously and, like her, had cowered under the tower of despair that had, at that time, loomed over him.

Later in the evening, after finishing her salsa class, Hilary arrived at her door and rummaged through her handbag for her keys. Her eyes suddenly spotted something on the doorstep. A single red rose. She hesitantly stooped low and picked it up in disbelief. Where had it come from? Who had left it? There was no note. *It can't be for me*, she told herself. She glanced around to see if there was anybody loitering in the street. The street was empty and the lamplights mocked the nothingness of night by dribbling rain from its blanket of black. She tenderly inhaled the delicate fragrance. The silken petals curled outwards, searching for life. Hilary eventually discovered her keys, unlocked her front door and stepped inside. She gently placed the single red rose carefully in her Portmeirion specimen vase and stepped back, staring at it, still in disbelief.

The next week was just as vacant as every other, but when Hilary reached her door after her salsa class, there was another red rose on the doorstep. This continued for four weeks until Hilary found herself rushing home in anticipation to see if there was another flower of love awaiting her. She became, over time, quite girlie and giggled at the sheer sight of a rose.

Her mind became filled with thoughts of who her secret admirer might be. After being married for so long and losing her husband, she had not really noticed the men passing her by in the street, but now she began observing them in earnest and glancing at them quizzically. Some smiled back, probably pitying the crazy woman with confusion etched across her face. She began investing in herself and made an appointment with the hairdressers to have her hair dyed back once again into a rich chestnut colour and shaped into a bob. Hilary began using make-up on her face. She daubed a mint-green eyeshadow on her eyelids and began painting her lips with her favourite Clinique 'Poppy Pop' red lipstick. Her elasticated black polyester trousers were replaced with fitted black jeans. What was she thinking of at her age? she asked herself, as she sprayed her Clinique Aromatics Elixir perfume over her blouse.

Had the widower across the road who always said good morning to her left the roses, or the gardener who always smiled at her when he was cutting Mrs Dobbs' front lawn? Hilary also began wearing her best red coat and suddenly found herself slipping her feet once again into her black high-heeled shoes, which she normally only wore for special occasions.

She continued popping into the corner shop for bits and pieces. Eric detected the spring in Hilary's step and – fettered by the faint glimmer of light in her eyes – observed how she seemed to be seeing the world differently. One day, feeling uncomfortable, he hid his face when she entered the shop and fumbled under the counter whilst trying to retrieve her newspapers. He coughed loudly before composing himself and, glancing up, hesitantly commented on how smart she was looking. Hilary blushed slightly.

The roses were still arriving and how she longed for Saturday to arrive.

In McCarthy and White, the estate office across town, Kevin tossed a glance at his mate, Kegan.

'How's your sister?' he quizzically asked.

'What?' replied Kegan vacantly, his eyes glued to his computer whilst watching the prices of properties escalate.

'Your sister.'

'Why?' snapped Kegan.

'Has she mentioned the roses I sent her?'

'What the Hell are you on about?'

'Well, I've been putting a red rose on her doorstep once a week when she was out at her yoga classes. I told you I was going to leave them, but I thought she would have mentioned them by now. You could have told her who they were from.'

'Oh, that. Didn't know you were serious,' replied Kegan, thoughtlessly.

'Maybe she's never received them, or she's blown me out before we've got started?' Kevin queried.

'Or has her dickhead husband come back on the scene?'

'Where were you sending them, Kev?'

'Twelve Beaumont Close, like you said.'

'No, no, you plonker. I said: Twelve Beaumont Road.'

'Oh God,' says Kevin

'Who the Hell's been getting them?'

Hilary tottered down the road to the corner shop. Eric caught sight of Hilary and once again shuffled with the newspapers under the counter. Why had he had put on his new blue checked Marks and Spencer's shirt to work in? He had no idea. He cleared his throat as she opened the door. 'It is so lovely to see you again, Mrs Albright.' A smile that tiptoes across his face dwelled a little longer, but the words he wanted to say were shelved like the jars of boiled sweets surrounding him. Hilary once again blushed slightly and, with a sudden parting of her lips, also found her words retreating. The shop became silent as they withdrew into their own space. The air, picking up angel dust, broke into a fine mist as the sun peeped through the buttress of cloud and tossed its light through the windows, and in a dreamlike moment, their eyes met across the counter with a special language all of their own.

In a twist of fate, love can be strange.

THE GIVER, THE TAKER, THE MISERY-MAKER.

Edna scuffs a few scattered telltale crumbs of toast quickly under the kitchen table with her stained fluffy slippers. She takes a sideways glance over her heavy-rimmed glasses at the faded cuckoo clock. A spring pings calling ten o'clock. No cuckoo; it had long escaped. She nestles into her macabre throne of steel and wheels.

There is a rustle by the front door and a clatter of keys. The door creaks open and she hears the strained chirruping call from her daughter.

'Hi, Mum, it's me.'

Jean makes her way into the kitchen and stoops to quickly kiss the frowning forehead of her mother. Edna does not move and stares ahead with a stolid determination, refusing to uncurl her bones.

'Have you managed to get any breakfast or shall I get you something?' Jean says in her shrill voice, which is a little too high for comfort.

'I haven't eaten since last night so I'll have some Weetabix and a mug of tea,' replies Edna.

Jean plods to the kitchen worktop, aware of the lack of 'please' at the end of her mother's sentence. With a lingering sigh, she puts the kettle on, busying herself as best she can.

Jean shivers a little in the bitterness of the room and adjusts the biscuit-beige cardigan drooping over her shoulders.

'How are we feeling today, Mum?' she gingerly asks, hiding her indifference.

'Still got my aches and pains, but I will have to live with them. It's alright for you, but it's been forty years since your father died, and what with my osteoarthritis, it has not been easy. Still, I will just have to soldier on.' A blanket of guilt wraps around Jean because her husband is still alive, but why? If only her mother knew.

Jean places the Weetabix, tea and spoon before her mother. A genie rises from the piping hot mug and floats to the ceiling, euphoric in his release.

'Where are my sweeteners? You know I can't drink my tea without my sweeteners. You are always moving them,' snaps Edna, tightening her thin receding lips.

'Here they are, Mum,' replies Jean in her resigned voice and places them next to her mother.

The doorbell chime pierces the air and Jean dejectedly drags herself out into the hallway. She opens the door and in rushes a care worker. Jean has seen her before. She is a rotund girl called Paris. *What a name for a girl who probably has never moved outside of Bristol*, thinks Jean. Paris bubbles with all the naivety and anticipation of assuming there is a wonderful life ahead of her. She pauses to put a scrunch in her bleach-frizzled hair and zigzags around the sad, dark brown fifties furniture like a fluttering bat.

'Gosh, there's so much clutter 'ere, me luver. You could fall ass over tits,' she fizzes.

Jean shudders. 'Paris, isn't it?' she politely asks.

'Yep,' replies Paris.

'What a lovely name. Have you been to Paris?'

'Nop. That's where that gert big tower is, innit? I've been to Alton Towers, though, with them big rides,' ponders Paris.

Jean smiles inwardly. Paris bends down to Edna and grasps the old lady's wizened hand, covered in tiny bunches of purple grapes, and strokes it tenderly.

''Ow are we today, darlin'?' she purrs to Edna. 'Well, got to get crackin'. Lots of old munters to see to today. Let's get you to the baffroom and get you scrubbed.'

Jean silently passes the newly washed polyester floral dress she had just taken out of her shopping bag to the helper. Jean glances at her mother, who, by some miracle, was trying to force a smile at Paris. Her frozen face had cracked slightly and her hollow eyes flickered with a spark of fire.

Edna, in her wheelchair, and the helper disappear into the bathroom. Jean hears the whispers and chuckling seeping out from under the door. Both of them in their secret world, whilst she is, once again, shut out.

Jean slumps into a vacant chair after making another drink and wipes her bone-pale face with her hand, then slowly runs her fingers through her peppered hair. She feels the beginnings of a headache rattling behind her right eye. A lifetime of being in attendance to an ungrateful mother has taken its toll. Jean tried to grasp happiness with both hands, but her mother's misery always hung like a heavy cloud, dragging her down. Jean feels the hopelessness of a loving relationship that, as far back as she can remember, has never materialised. She has never felt a loving mother's touch and feels like a ghost wandering in her invisibility through the stupidity of time.

There was really only one person in her mother's life and that was herself, followed by her golden boy. *No wonder Dad died earlier than he should have with a heart attack. He was not a husband, just another attendant*, ponders Jean.

The door of the bathroom flings open and the care worker pushes Edna into the room on her black chariot. Edna gives a backward glance at Jean over her shoulder and snaps, 'When you do my shopping this afternoon, can you add digestive biscuits to my list? I need them.'

'Yes, Mum,' replies Jean.

The care worker looks quizzically at Jean, who, by now, has her arms crossed to keep herself safe in the sanctity of her own space. Jean senses Paris is trying to work out the relationship between mother and daughter and probably thinks she is cold and unfeeling. Paris looks at Edna and says she has to go as time is precious. She squeezes Edna's hand with affection.

'Bye, me luver.'

Jean shows her to the door.

'Your Mu' is such a sweetie,' Paris says patronisingly.

Jean slams the door behind Paris and takes a deep breath, wishing she had all of her life ahead of her.

Suddenly, the back door is thrown open and in storms Jean's brother. He makes a beeline for his mother

'Hi, Mu', 'ow bist?' He stoops to put his arm around his mum and gives her a big hug, swallowing her up with his huge frame. 'Sorry I ain't been for a few weeks, but you know how fings are with work and the likes.'

'That's alright, my love. I know you work hard, sweetheart,' coos Edna.

Jean is pushed into silence and glances at her balding brother. His tattoos spill out from his short-sleeved dusty T-shirt, emblazoned with 'Ark at Ee'. He turns to Jean

'Hi, Sis, any chance of a brew?'

Jean plods once more into the kitchen.

'I haven't forgotten about the sticking back door, our Mu', but you knows time is precious. By the way, you 'aven't got a tenner I could scrounge? I've left my wallet at 'ome and 'ave to buy some tucker.'

'OK, my love, my purse is there on the sideboard. Help yourself,' Edna replies tenderly.

Jean bangs her brother's tea down on the table, spilling a little. 'I've put your three spoons of sugar in, so don't ask,' she snaps.

Jean watches her brother stuff more than one note into his back pocket. *The only food the ageing part-time security officer consumes will be liquid at The Bear and Rugged Staff,* thinks Jean.

Ian gulps the tea down and makes a hasty retreat.

'It is so nice of our Ian to come and see me. He is such a good lad,' witters Edna.

Jean makes her mother another mug of tea. 'Don't worry about the sweeteners. I have already put them in for you,' she says with a slight tremble in her voice.

'Anything else you want me to do before I leave, Mum?' asks Jean. 'I will pop in around three after I have done the shopping.'

'Good,' snaps Edna as she sips her tea 'I want to have a shut eye now and don't slam the door.'

'OK, Mum.' Jean obediently leans down to kiss her mother's cheek and Edna turns away.

Jean shuts the door softly behind her and lightly taps her feet along the cold shadows of the pavement towards her empty home. Menacing spits of rain mock the weariness of the day. She passes a litter bin and reaches into her pocket for the empty sleeping tablet bottle, which she smashes into its shocked mouth. Her feet feel lighter and do not falter but lead her on.

Edna, in the silence of her home, springs from her wheelchair.

'Thank goodness Jean's gone! I can make myself another piece of toast,' she triumphantly says to herself.

She makes her way, unaided, to the toaster but suddenly feels peculiar. Her legs buckle and the room spins. She sinks to the floor; this time, it is real. She screams for Jean in desperation, but Jean has long gone.

The loneliness of the room closes in and swallows up the misery-maker.

PANTOUM

THE HALL CLOCK STRIKES ONE

A lonely emptiness yawns and glues itself to my troubled walls,
In the silent vacancy of the stretched-out dimness of day.
Again, the hall clock strikes one, and smashes against the shores of my mind,
And echoes trample with weighted feet upon my icy weathered lanes of woes.

In the silent vacancy of the stretched-out dimness of day,
The brittle force of another amplified hour snaps within my empty room,
And echoes trample with weighted feet upon my icy weathered lanes of woes.
In the bleakness of my solitude, I grow weary of my own company.

The brittle force of another amplified hour snaps within my empty room,
Whilst sour shadows keep pace upon my tortured mind's imperfections.
In the bleakness of my solitude, I grow weary of my own company.
The ticking hours arrive late and brutal, marching their way towards death.

Whilst sour shadows keep pace upon my tortured mind's imperfections,
A lonely emptiness yawns and glues itself to my troubled walls.
The ticking hours arrive late and brutal, marching their way towards death.
Again, the hall clock strikes one, and smashes against the shores of my mind.

THE INJURED BIRD

A Saturday parcel stained by unanswered words,
Folded its way through the gaping mouth,
Of a letterbox.
Smacked by the coldness of the world,
A baby boomer bird,
Thrown from the comfort of her nest,
Into the chaos plopped.
Falling featherless down a funnel,
Scalded by frosty burns of interlocked genes,
The shrivelled fledgling,
In her premature weakness,
Winged her way through the swells,
Of blood-curdling rhynes.
The umbilical cord was butchered,
Well before birth.
Fate dealt out his hand and misfortune won,
No rising of a precious son,
From the depths of the earth.
In a cloakroom of echoes,
No room at the inn,
Amongst moth-balled hung jackets,

Perfumed to death,
A Cancerian was born,
With her crust eggshell thin.
Her wafer skin sighed,
With the faintness of breath.
Mother thrilled to the pain,
In the glory of gore,
She howled to the moon, although afternoon,
Relishing the fear.
The leading lady played her role,
She birthed and took the floor.
Mutagen milk from the martyr's breast,
Dried like a soured tear.
I grew not in spirit,
And learnt to survive,
And flew with my back to the rain.
But sometimes heard,
Is the sweetest trill, of joy,
In the softening of pain.

HAIKU

THE LONELY TOAD

Bulbous-eyed, I croaked.
Amongst the lonely shadows,
The dark silence spoke.

PANTOUM

THE LONELY VOYAGE

In violation, a cold wind storms across my tormented sails.
A heaving tide leaves its spittle of curses splattered upon the shores of my mind.
Drowning once more, in a loveless state, I contemplate my suicide,
As distressed waters smash over the shipwrecks of my past relationships.

A heaving tide leaves its spittle of curses splattered upon the shores of my mind.
Pernicious spirits hover above my bed to blunt my world,
As distressed waters smash over the shipwrecks of my past relationships,
Life's repugnant truths breach the restless shallows of my sleep.

Pernicious spirits hover above my bed to blunt my world.
With contempt, my ugly future stares through the portholes at my fate.
Life's repugnant truths breach the restless shallows of my sleep,
And awaiting my destruction, night terrors drop anchor into the deep darkness.

With contempt, my ugly future stares through the portholes at my fate.
In violation, a cold wind storms across my tormented sails,
And awaiting my destruction, night terrors drop anchor into the deep darkness.
Drowning once more, in a loveless state, I contemplate my suicide.

FREE VERSE

THE MADNESS OF MEN AND A POET

Alone, I sit with my grievances,
Which I select from my episodic memory.
I attempt to find a way of saying something,
When, alas, I have nothing really more to say.
All the lights in my life have been snuffed out.
All the egotistical men that came my way,
Owed their satanic pleasures, to my pain.
I still await, however, in my naivety, a miracle.

Trapped within my own isolation,
My raddled brain grasps for an understanding,
Of why men have such a penchant for self-gratification,
And are void of deep emotions like women.
From their wire-drawn lips
The words 'I love you'
Roll across their salacious tongues,
With no attachment to the real meaning.

Barren vows blow across women's aching hearts,
Their punishments are taken in silence and tears.
Without thought or consequence,
Men's words are shallow as the grave.
They say what needs to be said,

To achieve their pleasures,
And store those benign words,
Within the capacity of their limited love channels.

In the bleak dark space, I devour,
I plant my verse with every naked thought,
And watch the night's ticking hours,
Drag themselves towards the dawn.
I yawn, as the intensity of my man-hate,
Dances around my lonely room.
With the twist and curl of each word,
My imagination runs rampant.

Armed with resentment,
And not wanting to,
Once again, be the victim,
This poet in her madness,
Continues to write about life's torments,
And the mockery made,
Of her bleeding heart.
Whilst searching for love's domain.

Once more bruised and battered,
In my despondency,
I hold out my wanton arms,
To lovingly embrace,
In my inconceivable madness,
The tainted words of love,
From the grinning mouths,
Of mindless, self-deluded men.

THE MECHANICS OF LOVE

Although uncomfortable and troubled, I quietly wallow in the skill of doing nothing, absolutely nothing, until I spy her out of the corner of my eye at a distance and quickly slam my visor lids shut. Even the shot of morphine administered a few minutes ago cannot extinguish the searing pain I feel of seeing her in full flight. My warthog in clacking stilettos marches forward with her bleached hair piled high on her head like a Mr Whippy ice cream on a cone – minus a chocolate flake, I might add. She sweeps down the corridor of the hospital like a strong shoreward wind. I sense her overpowering presence as she gets closer. The air changes course and becomes spiked with tension as I feel her eggy breath whip across my face like coarse sand flogging a dune.

"Well, George, don't pretend you are asleep. I can tell you're not by your puckered eyelids."

I open one squinting secret eye and precariously focus on the forceful figure looming over me and notice the black thorny growth of whiskers on her chin, pointing mockingly in my direction. Is her beard in stark competition with mine? *Who is this woman?* I wonder. It's not the beauty I married thirty years ago. I study in depth the dark frets tracking across her exploding face, which fill me with a foreboding. I open up the other gloom-filled eye in defeat and, wiping some motes of road dust from my peppered beard, let out a long sigh, awaiting the crushing blow of her sonorous words.

"What the Hell have you been up to? They say you've broken your leg. A doctor informed me that you'll need a three-hour operation tomorrow. I'm so furious I could break your bloody neck as well." Her words spill forth, frothing and bubbling like a witch's cauldron. "What happened, George? And I want the truth for once."

"Well, love…"

My head spins like a drum, searching for excuses. I attempt to reply but meaningless words rattle around in the empty tank of my mouth and are too frightened to escape. Jean butts in.

"You were with her, weren't you, George? You sneakily went out with her behind my back, and you thought I wouldn't find out, but I did."

I watch Jean's jaw pump up and down like a well-oiled piston.

"How old are you, George? You're much too decrepit for her. What's she got that I haven't?"

The list would be endless, so I let the draughty gap of my silence do the talking.

"Well, love, is she OK?" I flippantly ask, trying to hide my consternation, and toss Jean a rigid grin.

"Don't call me love! She is your only love. You've made that clear, going behind my back."

"A car pulled out from the side turning like we were invisible and hit us side on. Typical, just typical. Drivers seldom bother to look nowadays," I reply, endeavouring to hatch a weak excuse.

"Anyway, seeing you're so interested in her, she was lucky – more's the pity. The police told me that she escaped with only minor scratches, not like you, you bugger," scowls Jean.

I let the crude oil wash over me and yearn for the pleasures of a more refined lubrication. I let the vision of my real love drip into the crevices of my imagination. I grasp at a moment of peace between the onslaught of Jean's artillery of words and slam my lids shut, allowing the drone of Jean's voice wittering on about my indiscretions, being thirsty, and the urgency of a cup of coffee evaporate into the distance. I suck at the barbed air as I take up arms with my inner self. Should I relinquish my heart and finish with my romance and remain faithful to my wife? Will my head win over my heart? No chance. Everything important in life cannot be seen by the naked eye and I know in this briefest spilling of time that fate will eventually reunite me with the young swarthy body of my real love. I breathe a wanton sigh. I open my eyes once again to the stark harshness of reality and the uncompromising figure at my bedside, casting her long shadow.

"Do you know where she is now, Jean?" I enquire, with an urgency for compassion. I wait for Jean's tongue to wind up and let go.

"She is where she should be. Someone has taken her home. Home is where I want her to stay. Why did you take her out when I begged you not to have anything more to do with her? We've had this conversation time and time again."

Jean will not let go of the throttle.

"Why can't you leave her alone? She has become your obsession. I am fed up, I tell you, fed up with playing second fiddle."

"Can you scratch my toes? They itch."

"No."

"Thanks a lot."

Her mouth steps up into fifth gear. "You have to make your mind up, George. It is either her or me, and I mean it this time. Our marriage is too crowded with the three of us in it."

Jean, like a medicine man casting his spell, rattles her fist above my chest. I feel the chill of her screwdriver eyes winding down deep inside of me into the dark flooded caverns of my soul as she hunts for the harshness of the truth. I lay fettered in the headlights of her glare. I glance up at her tight mouth, made uglier by its anger. I know over the years the rosebud lips I longed to kiss have been starved by the absence of mine, and now, like wilting leaves, curl downwards.

My judge has passed her sentence and out comes the black cloth. I attempt to manoeuvre the conversation by pressing hard on the footbrake to divert another accident of the mouth. I turn over the frayed fabric of my thoughts.

"They've cut off my new jeans. I only bought them from M&S last week. Twenty-six quid, they cost me."

"Serves you right," slams Jean. "And don't ask me for some more money to bail you out. I know what you've spent on her. I'm not a fool."

"Never said you were, love," I reply with a dusting of sarcasm.

"How long do you think it will be until you're out and about after the operation?" asks Jean, with a sudden, unsuspecting hint of softness.

"God knows," I reply.

"I won't be dancing in attendance to you, let's get that straight. Do you hear me?" replies Jean, her tongue dipped in vinegar.

"Yes, yes, I can hear you loud and clear. I don't expect you to do anything for me; why change a habit of a lifetime?" I snap back but feel a hint of impending doom because I know I am chained like a sprocket and will need her assistance. I have lost control of my life. How I yearn to be free from all the shackles and trappings of our union so I can capture my youth and once again feel the blast of wind rushing through my hair. However, my rocky road towards an open gateway has always been blocked by the cones of commitments and the unrelenting chaos that spills across my path from the hard shoulder of marriage. Travelling down the highway of life, I know my wife and I are not going in the same direction.

"Can you pass me my leather jacket on the chair? I need my mobile in the pocket," I beg and use an insubstantial 'please' at the end of my sentence for protection.

Jean flings it at me forcefully. "What do you want the phone for? I'm here and she can't speak to you." Her mouth opens and shuts like a 7000rpm tappet. Spreadeagled, the jacket smashes itself into my chest like a dying crow shot from the sky.

"Watch my bad leg, for God's sake!" I snap at her.

My sprawling blackbird surrenders itself to me. I bought the studded jacket when I first encountered my sweetheart. I remember the day well. It's etched on my brain. I recall the alloyed joy of seeing the soft silken lines of my beautiful woman's body through the showroom window. She was with another man and he was listening to the accelerated purr of her dulcet tones. Jealousy overpowered me as I watched my enemy grin in the comfort of her company and stray his greasy finger over her nipple. Her golden name was tattooed on her ample breast, taunting me. Like a man possessed, my thighs ached with the urgency to mount her and my heart was brimming with the insanity of my infatuation. Is it an atrocity to love too much? What is true love? I knew there and then this balding born-again biker had to buy her – the love of his life, the Triumph Thunderbird.

THE MYSTICISMS OF LIFE

Mystical flossy forms float,
Through different dimensions.
Destabilised in abandonment,
Spectres search in monochrome mists,
For the once rigid organisation of life.

They hunger for lost boundaries,
Which kept them unthinking and safe.
Stabilised structures of false realities,
Have slipped through their grasp,
And have dissipated into the ether.

The tenebrous days of war are over,
The fears they face are imbalances.
Plasma-constructed greys,
Conceptualise the surroundings,
They find themselves in.

Their liberation takes on a haunting.
Reasoning slips through their grasp.
Each fractured shape,
Searches for calm in the chaos,
And hunts out its own rigid boundaries,

To quell the fear of freedom,
Is a completely new complexity,
The few survivors face.
Paradoxically, they exonerate themselves,
From the previous damage caused.
In the wanton destruction,
For greed and power,
The profound implications,
Were not realised until too late,
With the destabilisation of their world.

Lifeless, the mute figures wander,
In exile upon the scorched earth,
Searching for the deepest truths,
Each with a different perspective,
Of what went outrageously wrong.

With outstretched fingers,
In the heavy hung mists
The seditious souls,
Search for a new understanding of life.
To quell their disorientated minds.

Amongst the tundra of truth,
Alas, it is too late,
Iridescent dreams for the future,
Lay in ashes at their feet,
And, like an echo, out of reach.

THE PERPETUAL WINTER

Tangled anaemic sinews skim,
Across the cursing mouth,
Of gelid skies.
Brittle-boned boughs
Crack and snap,
Displacing harmonious notes,
Within the cacophony of sound.
Fearful frozen flocks huddle,
Glued ghostly together,
Against the bare twigs,
And mish-mash of mesh,
Which defends each
Unshaven bristled field.
The unforgiving land
Tightens its grasp,
And throttles the throats,
Of underground dishevelled roots.
Mucus gobs of greyish phlegm,
Cling to defiant sprout stalks.
A fretwork of frosty trapped tears,
Line the hopelessly lost ruts,
And fleece squatting carcasses
Of tractors, eaten to death
With rust and corrosion.

A swinging untamed gate,
Clatters and cries out its grievances
To the gnawing wind.
Hard-hearted bone stones,
Holding their own resentment,
Devour the scene,
Dictating the lonely path,
Where I ploughed my own furrow.
Winter holds no pity
Within its petrified hands.
The wind screeches with laughter,
At the frozen sod of my demise,
And my unseeded frigid heart,
Which is unable to harness love.
Praying for the shift of seasons,
I seek shelter from winter's icy will.
Tortured by the weather,
And chilled by the cold,
Perpetual bleakness of life,
Snail-like, beggar stooped, I stumble.

Amongst the turbulent squall,
My footprints slowly dissipate,
And a nothingness remains,
Upon the snowy barren fields of life.

THE POSTURING OF PAULA

Paula announced with pride that she was going to become vegan. It arrived like a defiance, out of the ether.

She always loved her meat but informed me she was not going to eat any animal products. How could she turn vegan, I asked myself, when she always loved her meat?

Paula belonged to a one-parent family, consisting of me and her younger brother, Rob. No other siblings, they both live with their daft mother – me.

My daughter and I had always been so close and confided in each other. Paula was a normal average teenager, bringing her many mates around to our home. Music blaring from the bedroom was the norm. Posters of bare-chested handsome men adorned the walls of her bedroom. Many I wouldn't have minded having around for a coffee! I would always hear Paula and her mates giggling and chatting from the confines of her bedroom. Yes, there was a definite happiness that reverberated within the cosy walls of my home.

The girls all looked similar; dyed blonde hair past their shoulders, long multicoloured glittered fingernails, eyelashes you could sweep the floor with and skirts so short that they were definitely not within the realms of decency.

Life continued much the same. I worked hard as a carer to make ends meet, but making sure I spent as much of my spare time with Paula and Rob as I could.

As the months progressed, I began seeing little changes in Paula. She didn't want to go shopping or have coffee with me as she usually did. Her many friends drifted away and slowly she became more insular. Her dress habits changed. She stopped wearing her high heels and bought Doc Martens black ankle boots. The short skirts were replaced with baggy tartan and grey trousers. Her fingernails were cut short. I noticed little differences. When wearing sleeveless T-shirts, I noticed she did not shave her armpits anymore. Nor did she wear any cosmetics. I did tentatively bring up the subject and was tersely told she would not wear slap to pay homage to any man. She studied my expression, which I managed to keep frozen. I tried to dismiss my concerns at the change in her, but to keep peace and to keep a close bond, I kept my opinions to myself, until one day she arrived home with her hair cropped brutally short and dyed back to her natural colour, a mousey brown. I gasped in shock as she marched through the back door.

'Oh my God, Paula! What have you done?'

'What do you mean?' she snapped back and threw me one of her black looks, which often arrived bare-headed, my way.

I found myself initially too nervous to say anything, but, summoning up courage, I muttered, 'You have changed your style, my darling – not that I mind, but it is a shock, Paula sweetheart, as it is as short as Rob's.'

'And while we are on the subject, Mother' (she never called me 'Mother'), 'I wish to be known from now on as Paul.'

I froze on the spot and felt like my legs were going to give way. I was struck dumb. Processing the changes in my daughter had been difficult, but because of my love for my daughter, I had to let my biased reasoning flow in a different channel. I found it difficult to recognise the truthful shores now facing me in my life.

'OK,' I quietly replied in defeat. I could not afford to argue with her and lose one of the loves of my life.

I turned around and, weeping gently, made my way to my bedroom, lost in the shallows of my misunderstanding.

As the months progressed, all of Paula's – or should I say Paul's – friends disappeared, except for a new butch friend she bought to the house named 'Del'. Del had sour features and was quite daunting, as she stomped around my house like she owned the place. I was not going to take that assertive person on. I kept quiet as a mouse, accepting everything that came my way, just to keep a closeness with my daughter.

I attempted to make conversation with Rob even though he spent most of his time in his bedroom, but he did not want to get involved with his sister and just shrugged his shoulders in silence at my questioning.

A few months back, he sauntered into the kitchen to have his breakfast and I noticed he was wearing blue nail varnish! Nail varnish! My heart skipped a beat, although I am being schooled by my children on being yourself whatever the consequences. I consoled myself that at least it was blue. Blue for boys, how ridiculous was that! But I could not go down the winding path of another one of my child's self-identification issues, as my life was rocky enough.

As time marched on, I was educated on many subjects by Paul, including the many lettered identities nowadays such as LBTQSWJFRZY. Bloody alphabet! Not sure what it was all about but tried to nod in the right places and show that I understood, which I didn't. I am of the old school, which thinks there are only two genders – male and female. Shows how old-fashioned I am.

I was also educated on English. I thought English was my best subject at school but I soon realised that I knew nothing about pronouns!

A year has passed since the gradual change in my Paul and I am resigned to whatever life throws at me. I often ponder on the question: How can I change the old conditioned me? My ageing pug, Bruce, staggers into the kitchen to be fed. He looks at me, begging for food. *Maybe he wants to be a budgie*, I tell myself. *Maybe I should put some bird seed in his dog bowl.*

Standing at the kitchen worktop, I prepare the family's supper. *Thank goodness my daughter is back to eating meat.* I lay out mine and Rob's roast dinner, then stretch up to get a saucer down from the cupboard and chop little pieces of chicken into it for her, before placing it firmly on the floor next to her scratch post and much-loved green velvet mouse.

I dare Bruce to eat it. He looks quizzically at me but does not move. It is as if he knows it is the cat's dinner.

'Darling,' I call out, 'your food is ready!'

THE REAL ME

I wear my hold-ups ten denier and glossy,
And carry an air of don't care, and quite bossy.
I colour my pain with cosmetic paint,
And wear four-inch heels to show what I ain't.
Whenever I float between sleep and awake,
I shut my lids tight as life is so fake.
I don't give a damn about what's going on,
But I sing from the sheets a normality song.
I exist in the shallows of pretence,
Too frightened to fall off the fence.
I remember to nod in all the right places,
When confronted with seas of bored lifeless faces.
Branded the poor widow, who is the sadder?
You might think I'm sane, but beware I am madder!

THE SANCTUARY

In violation,
I pick over his privacy.
4 x 2s essential,
Every man has to have them.
Never know when needed.

Assortment of dusty overalls,
Hang from rusty nails,
Like tired ghosts on gallows.
Stains cling like testaments,
To testosterone and long-lost skills.

Half-empty rusty tins of paints,
Harden like my heart.
Rainbow colours, no further use,
My world is painted over
With magnolia.

Ladders, different sizes,
Rungs, rotted by time,
Lean effortless to the walls,
Not leading to Heaven,
Not leading anywhere in particular.

A worn leather bag,
Holding imperial tools,
Keeps its zipped mouth shut,
Concealing its demise,
Of bygone sizes.

Webs hang precariously,
From roof, devouring the space.
Half-opened seed packets,
With unfulfilled promises,
Lay faded along with good intentions.

Many tools without recognition,
Make a mockery of my limitations.
Vernier Caliper, familiar name,
Imprinted on my addled brain,
But, sadly, cannot place its face.

The dust sucks at the oil-stained floor,
Where his bike bled and died,
Trapped within its own isolation.
Tins of polish line makeshift shelves,
Not used to lustre dull lives.

Tyres, wheels,
Michelin, Bridgestone,
Rolling rubber stones propped on walls.
Patterns, opposing treads,
Never tried and tested the tarmac.

Heavy spades, forks, shears,
Accentuate my poor health.
I feel the confines of age,
And its wearisome chains,
Restricting me from gardening life.

I sigh as realisation strikes,
I must let go of his slavery,
The urgency to acquire.
Memories, dipped in grief,
Taunt my travel to the savage tip.

In the hopelessness of life,
And sealing myself inwards,
I unload, with good intentions,
His loving treasures,
Into the gaping satanic steel mouths.

OCTOSYLLABIC VILLANELLE.

THE SILENT TEAR

With outstretched hands, I touch the fear,
my fractured heart's shattered in two,
the saddest is the silent tear.

A smog of pain hangs low, won't clear,
I trawl the mist, but where are you?
With outstretched hands, I touch the fear.

My future's grey ash blows so near,
I need your arms, what can I do?
The saddest is the silent tear.

The landscape of your smile appears,
I cannot face the final truth,
with outstretched hands, I touch the fear.

My calling fell upon deaf ears,
I thought we were the chosen few,
the saddest is the silent tear.

My wanting rides the night that jeers,
despair's an arch my life twists through.
With outstretched hands, I touch the fear,
the saddest is the silent tear.

HAIKU

THE SLAUGHTER

*In the war's slaughter,
He used all his willpower,
To pray to the sky.*

THE SWORD OF DAMOCLES

The sword of Damocles hung heavy above our heads,
'How long?' my husband's migrant voice asked,
In heaving tones. 'Weeks, months or years?'
Another wrinkle pencilled itself boldly across my brow.
I awaited in anticipation, the specialist's answer.
He cast his eyes downwards to the uneasy floor.
He sucked at the air and, with a withering smile,
Choked on his mucus-weighted words,
Fossilising under the low-ceilinged room.
'I'm afraid weeks,' the specialist stammered,
Exposing his lugubrious personality.
Husband lowered his eyes, defeated in battle.
I gave my clumsy tears the power to roam,
over the lonely shores of my sunken cheeks.
My husband ambushed his insuperable thoughts,
Whilst intransigently holding onto his space.
Knowing irrefutably, he could not defer his death,
He understood he would soon face his maker.
Before the snuffing out of his living light,
As the room spilt its bone-bare walls upon my love,
And anchored him to the spot with chains of damnation,
He knew with certainty he would front his death with dignity.
Rising resolutely, he held out his firm hand towards me.
In my repressed rage, I stretched out my shaking fingers,
Weeping selfishly at the loathing of my future.

THE TORMENT OF TIME

The grandfather clock strikes three and jeers from the coldness of the hallway. *One, two, three,* Bill counts, whilst listening intently to the foreboding echoes slapping themselves against the crispy crumble-coloured walls. At a drunken pace, time staggers towards him. Bill fidgets in his armchair and his downcast eyes notice the splashes on his blue tartan slippers. A crude cuss escapes from the sanctuary of his dribbling mouth. He reaches in his cardigan pocket for his grubby hanky and swipes at the saliva, as, once again, with laboured breath, he snuggles under the branches of his thoughts, searching for escapism in the wasting of time, and places the rag back into his pocket.

He recalls the past pleasure of just sitting in the warmth of a coffee shop, listening to the incessant chattering of people, the clicking of cups whilst humans enjoyed themselves. The joy of socialising – a word that now has a distinct stain to it.

His eyes are drawn to the hostile drizzle dragging its tendons down the lounge window and catches sight of a few people, each lost in their fragility of thought. The straggling muzzled sheep sidestep one another in a dance of death, to avoid infection and attempt, without question, to obey their political dictators. He notices a small jittery damp dog being dragged along the pavement by its owner and is taken aback by the colour-coordinated muzzle of the owner and the neckerchief the dog is wearing. Maybe the dog really needs a matching muzzle instead? *The world has gone mad*, he tells himself. There is talk of people wearing two muzzles. Maybe we will eventually have to wear three and slowly suffocate ourselves. The stupidity makes Bill's lips curl slightly into a saccharine smile. Bill watches the folk outside from his well of loneliness and tastes their fear hovering in the air. FEAR, FEAR, the stick that controls us all. *Am I one of those conspiracy theorists?* he quizzes. *Have I still got some fight left in me? No, probably not, I'm brow-beaten Bill, married to Sheila for fifty years. Had to conform to what society expected; have to conform now. Fifty years of being the obedient, ambushed husband, listening to Sheila's incessant nagging.*

Bill once more loses himself in the grey mist surrounding the germination of his thoughts. Still, she was a habit he became accustomed to. Bill often feigned hard of hearing – Sheila's voice was more than any ear could hold – and he would often blank himself off and travel to faraway shores in his mind, which normality would not recognise. They both lived their lives tinged with death. Eventually, throughout the tides of time, they found themselves looking at one another out of the corners of their eyes with a shallow blankness as they circled one another like two fighters in a boxing ring, waiting to see who would land the first blow. Their lips grew thin and the colours of their lives turned beige, living within their pleasant form of misery. Although ebullience was a word that had deserted Bill many years ago, he discovered some sort of enjoyable boredom joining the local bowling club and having pints down the Rose and Crown. A game of darts would also brighten up a miserable evening. Now Covid-19 had snatched away any form of enjoyment as social gatherings were banned. Bill was trapped in a boredom bubble with Sheila. A bubble that he dreamed of bursting. She always had jobs for him to do. Lists and lists of them. Covid-19 had played right into her hands. His eyes wandered to his toolbox by the side of his well-worn armchair. At least he had mended the kitchen cupboard door as she had demanded and completed a few more minor jobs on her never-ending list, so he felt he was not all that disobedient.

The room grew darker; the clouds had gathered and dropped their grey guts over the house. Despondency had been, once again, fanned as the minutes crawled into the crevices of Bill's cell.

Bill's stomach began to rumble. He knew he should really make an effort before the shops closed to buy some food, but he did not want to robotically shuffle to the supermarket with a muzzle on and stare at a newly installed traffic-light system to see if he could enter. A rotund member of staff, drenched in his power of authority, with a sanitiser gun in his hand, would stare at him. And with a wire-drawn smile would size Bill up. Another victim to shoot. He would only usher him in when convenient. Bill then made the wild decision that he would not conform and give the smug cowboy the pleasure of acting out *High Noon*.

Bill gazes around the room and endeavours to spark an interest in something other than DIY. He spots Sheila's jigsaw puzzle. Who would want to remake the scene, time and time again, of a bloody yellow handcart nestled in trees, like Sheila? He stares at the pieces, knowing all he wanted to do was to slam them against the wall! He tells himself he will not put the lying BBC news on either. He knows it will fill his head with what they want him to believe. The vaccine, the vaccine. Bill recently had the flu, pneumonia and shingle jabs, and is determined not to be a pincushion again. Let the government officials be the guinea pigs for the first round of vaccines and if – *if* – in a couple of months, there are no side effects, then and only then will he consider it, he assures himself with steely determination. The news would be about the protesting students, anyway. And what is the problem with students? Let them have their Freshers Week, drink, take drugs and shag. *I would*, reflects Bill. *Oh, I would if I was young and wild again.* And what about the younger children? The poor buggers who can't see their school mates because the schools are shut and are probably penned in at home with bickering parents? Let the younger generation live! *I am eighty; I have had my time and if death comes beating its wings in the darkness to my door, then so be it*, he ponders. Death is only part of life. He knew in his heart of hearts his views were in opposition to most, but did he care?

Bill's fogbound thoughts journeyed towards religion. Although not a dedicated believer in what the church stood for, he felt he still had the right to escape to a church and have a quiet chat with God if he wished, even if God didn't want to listen to a whinging old man. Bill could not fathom out why churches were locked in everyone's hour of need. Reluctantly, he agreed that they should not be used for mass gatherings, but God is needed on your side when Covid-19 is lurking around every corner and ready to pounce. Surely it is not a time for the church to give up the ghost. It is a time for the kingdom of God to shine in all its radiant glory. Come on, God, man up!

The clock fiercely strikes the quarter hour and spreads its canker across the serenity of silence. The shadows continue playing hide-and-seek as the day turns inside out. The room begins to darken as the sky outside turns greyer. Bill fleetingly closes his eyes, hoping for the peace of sleep, just for a few minutes, to wipe away the aching loneliness of the hours.

Bill awakens with a start as the grandfather clock strikes the half hour. Its brass minute hand points downwards, attempting to show the world the drama that has played out. A shadowy shape of a gnarled hand clutching at the hall rug pokes out from the doorway and lays stiff and still. 'Bloody, bloody Covid. I tried to keep two metres apart from her,' Bill tells himself. 'I tried to convince her that is what we had to do, even though she insisted we were allowed to be in the same bubble. She wouldn't hear what I had to say and kept stepping into my hallowed space. It became too stifling and crowded for the two of us. It is all the virus's fault, not mine,' mumbles Bill convincingly. 'Suicide rates have doubled. Domestic violence, tripled. All because of these damn lockdowns.'

Bill leans sideways in his chair and, with his right hand, pulls out his creased hanky from his pocket. He stretches out his left hand to rummage in his toolbox and finally retrieves his dead-blow hammer. He once again swipes the head of it with his hanky, checking it is still void of bloodstains. Then, feeling he achieved a job well done, he places the hammer back in its rightful place as the hollow minutes mock.

THE TORMENTED TOAD

Squashed, I squat amongst the feculent swamps of my own making,
Like a pustule waiting to burst forth upon the wetness of earth's wounds.
Mantled in mists, like steam in a tagine, remote from happy,
I stare swollen-eyed into night's blindness, waiting for morning's misplaced light.

My croaks wander loud and deep as they travel in the direction of my fears,
And roll down the echoing corridors of my future's eternal emptiness.
With thoughts sealed inwards, my heart openly pulsates outside of itself.
Bloated, like a greedy man's distended belly, I await your pardon.

The rain cracks the dull mirrors of the marshes, exposing the truth.
Swaddled in reeds, taut and tall, where death creeps, I utter, 'Please love me, warts and all.'

THE WEATHER OF THE HEART

In the unpredictable weather of the heart,
In the cold, pitiless attrition,
A fluttering of memories silently drift.
Angels lay their snowy pinions,
Upon the unforgiving earth,
Of my mind,
To ease the insuperable pain.

Trapped in the bleak tenebrous days,
Of my deep midwinter, I shiver.
The rush of short days,
Catches my breath.
And in the ruins,
And the ticking tides of time,
I search for a release,
Amongst the cold strange light.

On the blank white pages,
Of frozen fields,
My lonely footprints,
Maybe spell out my fate.
The pages of my future,
Before me lay wordless.

The tyranny of frost,
Is apparent in my face.
I hold out my hand,
For the bud that must appear,
In the lap of spring's light.
I await the stretched-out days,
And the soft kisses of the sun.

I await in anticipation,
A new beginning, a new love.
In winter's bleakness,
Wrapped up in a scarf of himself,
My distant malapert man departs,
Along with the old year.

PARKINSON'S

Diagnosis: Parkinson's Disease.
Not enough tissues to contain my tears.
Fear of my deficiencies and fear of the unknown.
I fondle my glitter dance shoes.
Too afraid to let go of the past,
I hide them in the back of my wardrobe,
And within the darkest recesses of my mind.
I will have to dance the Parkinson's shuffle,
With all its clumsiness, from now on.
I bite my trembling lower lip, to take control,
Of my shuddering despair,
And to avoid the onslaught of pity.
Excess saliva gathers in the corners,
Of my smudged poppy-red lips,
Which I discretely wipe.
In the savage wilderness of the disease,
I search for solace between the stars.
Euphemisms are used to soften the blow,
Swallowed up in the torrent of questions that flow my way.
What will I achieve
Within the narrowing of my limited capacity channel?
With shaking hands, my creative writing
Becomes a tiny spider with tracery steps.
My shaky script, making no sense, dissipates.

I will, however, not be blotted from life's page.
And will not be defined as Parkinson's, not Julie.
Hunched back, I still stand tall,
And bend like the willow in the biting winds,
When my world around me shatters in the hellish squall.
Have I the forbearance to accommodate my new life?
That is an open-ended question.
Acid bare, I wander the lonely corridors,
Of what was once a lustred pathway.
Deep in the misalignments of my thoughts,
I remain raddled but still blessed to be me.

PANTOUM

THE WINGS OF DARKNESS

Words surceased in sorrow, lie waiting for the light.
Lines drawn in the sands of time chalk across the night.
In my vast void of darkness, I seek your fading face.
Sorrow flaps its wings in torment, beating the empty space.

Lines drawn in the sands of time chalk across the night.
The flight of your death clouds my eyes, and takes away my sight.
Sorrow flaps its wings in torment, beating the empty space,
Whilst ghostly figures haunt my pain, keeping up their pace.

The flight of your death clouds my eyes, and takes away my sight.
My tremulous frosts of woes, fill my heart with fright.
Whilst ghostly figures haunt my pain, keeping up their pace,
The features of your slanted smile, within the skies I trace.

My tremulous frosts of woes, fill my heart with fright.
Words surceased in sorrow, lie waiting for the light.
The features of your slanted smile, within the skies I trace.
In my vast void of darkness, I seek your fading face.

HAIBUN

TUMOURS

The excrescences appeared upon his body, and day by day he realised he had to chase his dreams away. The exuberance of his life had to be redacted. He visited the specialist with a fusillade of questions of which there were no answers. Each day, he persevered with his treatment. Life whorled out of control. The pressures of the crises were weighty. But…

In his quiet space,
He gave himself permission,
To hope for the best.

UNANSWERABLE TEARS

Ethereal memories in autumnal mists,
Slow their deathly pace,
As sharp winter blades cut my flesh,
I try to recall his heavenly face.
I moisten his ghostly grave with tears,
Falling like blinding rain.
Cloaked in misery, I sob,
In the summit of my pain.
With my heart as a hunter,
I wonder aloud about my destiny.
Wanton starved lips,
No more to be kissed,
A premonition of what will be?
A wind mocks the fleeting of the day,
And laughs at death through dying leaves,
Which dissipate in the worthless shadows,
And the wretchedness that winter heaves.
In my loneliness, who do I cry for?
Pray, my guides, tell me who?
For a love cut short in sorrowful times,
Or do I selfishly sob for myself,
And not you?

UNREQUITED LOVE

My snatched dreams are haunted.
Cold and shivering, I awaken,
Waiting for the light,
And wondering if I can ever love again?
I cannot mouth the words your ears long to hear.
My lips remain puckered, willing to kiss,
But I cannot oblige.
Instead, I rub smiles into your weeping wounds.
You drown in the storm of my eyes,
And remain deaf to my stabbing words of truth.
My unfinished poetry remains stranded,
Upon the unresolved pages within my brain.
As you turn away from this empty vessel,
A part of me longs to remain in your arms,
But that is my selfishness, searching for hugs.
Which, alas, adds to your torment.
This fragile butterfly, once again, beats her wings,
Against the frozen windows of her fate.
The disconnection, as always, remains between us,
As your heart circles the jealous Heavens.
Alas, my love cannot be demanded.
It is a gift I willingly give,
Securely wrapped,
In the supreme authority over my freedom.

SONNET

WATERWHEEL

Glass wings sparkle in the dizziness of an adrenalin rush,
and wasting time cavort in the continuum of the waterwheel.
Moistened lips spit their words in a glittering gush.
Crystal stars pep the skies in the spinning of the reel.

Fluid bones splice the rippling dimpled cheeks,
and rising spark the Heavens, tossing diamonds in the air.
Bubble eyes thaw the stream's icy gaze, sheeting the waters
with a soufflé of excitement that is ours to share.

The seasons track time, somersaulting over the mantle of the skies.
I whirl through spring's verdant optimism and summer's scented
   spin.
Grasping a moment that's mine, I reap the harvest of your quiet
   eyes,
before the bitterness of a biting winter rolls in.

We splash our toes in life's fast flow, kicking up a mist,
but who can tell when our river dries with the shrinking from
   a kiss?

WE ARE THE GREYS

Bulbous black fly-eyes spy,
In kaleidoscope sections.

Transported inquisitors mull over your minds,
Filled with imperfections,

And underdeveloped extrasensory perceptions.

Neanderthal man, you're cocooned,
With no constellation conception.

My sombre, cinereous-slate silken skin,
Concealed within a twilight zone.

Our almond Argus-eyes hunt in evenings,
On earth named home.

Observing your oblivion,
In the passing seas of sad humanoid faces,

We search out species for hybridisation,
To produce superior races.

Our transportation with extraterrestrial powers, makes its
  penetration.

Deciphering minor minds is our only communication,
With our miniscule mouths agape,
We stare with obsolete oration.

My evanescent being,
Is it all in vain,

Seeking a superior brain?

Chameleon cumbersome creatures,
With lumbering frames,
Overcrowded on their satirical star.
For scientific tests,
We undercover umbrageous agents,
Watch you from afar.

One by one vetted to be interconnected,
To open your conscious awareness.

Projected through space, the human race,
In saucer-shaped ships,
Their screams we suppress.

Who have travelled before?
Psychologists explore,
Abductees who choose not to believe.

With flashbacks of fear,
Of previous freak shows,
And metallic probes,
Panic returns amongst grief.

We silent figures that glide softly within,
Touch your albescent skins.
Perturbed mirrors of your soul remain vexed.

Experimental, non-incidental,
With elongated fingers, we elevate, interconnect and dissect.

Tears translucent well beneath limpid lids,
Of bodies bound,
Stifled into silence, no sound.

Data we store from banal beings on board,
Before your ejaculation down to the ground.

Embryos extracted for conception,
With your unawareness of deception.
Our expectation of integration,
bonding our species,
Hopes of no rejection.

Obliterated ozone,
Earth's destruction by pollutants,

Hopeful genetic engineering,
The rulers, interbred mutants.

You and I as one, the nightmare's begun,
Live in fear.

Your planet has died,
There is nowhere to hide,
Beware of the Greys, WE ARE HERE!

WEATHER PATTERNS

The day's bubbling cauldron erupts,
Cluttering the blue canvas,
With a composition,
Of cumulus clouds.
Parched scented floral lips uncurl,
Salacious tongues taste the air,
Searching for,
The unfulfilled promise of rain.

Our daily actions,
Are compromised,
And governed by the sun.
Deviations in weather patterns,
Can impede our hectic lives.
Making us realise,
Everything can suddenly change,
For better or for worse.

WEB OF DECEIT

A wizened old man sips his beer. His fingers trace a migratory scar trailing through his wispy hair. He peers blindly into the police office window opposite the pub, deep in thought.

Frank, a morose bugger, straddles the corner of his pockmarked cluttered desk, swinging his scuffed right carbon boot. He takes a long drag on his cigarette, leans his head back and menacingly blows a smoky halo.

"You don't need a halo where you're going, Frank," Linda mocks.

Frank and Linda duck their darts, with flights of loathing. Linda squealed on Frank five years previously, misconduct concerning a hit-and-run case. Frank bristles at the hard-hearted, blonde-haired Linda. She flirts in her mourning suit; her inviting ample bust gushes over the top of her starched white blouse, showing a hint of a hooker. Most fancy their chances, but Linda knows the testosterone office is just a junkie's vein, full of pricks. She is married, but that ranks low in her life.

"Here, run your eyes over this lot." She scatters the breadcrumbs of paper over Frank's desk, feeding her bird of prey on dregs of death.

With a defiant death rattle, Frank clears his throat. He hopes for chunks of succulent flesh he can sink his teeth into, not tiny morsels. Linda, who always had a grudging respect for Frank, ponders on what he will do after his retirement in a few weeks. His clothes reek of loneliness; a faded shirt, worn-out collar. The top button swings like a fallen trapeze artist hanging by a thread in his safety harness. A kedge-belly peeps from his shirt; forty years of fast foods and fat sugared doughnuts, oozing blood.

"We have to be seen to be going through the motions with this case, Frank, but it's only an old bloke."

The paragon of virtue, the pretender, dispassionately drifts through the door of the CID room. *I'm an old codger now*, he ponders.

Frank slides himself off the desk. He fingers inside his pocket and retrieves his worn snapshot of Rosie, taken from him three years into their marriage. Effervescent eyes gaze towards him, dark ringlets coil around a pallid face, pouting lips, too delicate to kiss. Roadkill Rosie; pickings on a tarmac platter for a murder of crows. Frank crumples into the weary weather-beaten leather chair, replacing the photo. Defeated, he thumbs through the post-mortem paperwork.

October 2010. William deceased, 85 years of age, discovered on bedroom floor. Second wife says he fell out of bed. Stepson says he fell down the stairs. A coroner's report states unnatural causes.

Examination
Elderly white male of small build. Abrasion over lower right flank 20 x 10mm. Abrasion on lateral right buttock/upper right thigh 20 x 20mm. Bruise on the posterior right forearm 90 x 70mm also laceration. The

right clavicle fractured 7cm from the sternoclavicular joint. Right third and sixth ribs both fractured posteriorly. Intrathoracic haemorrhage.

Frank lurches forward and reads on. Poor Bill smashed to pieces like a porcelain plate on a kitchen floor.

Frank makes some fleeting calls. The stale fug is buzzing with the hum of heartless homicides. A round-faced clinging clock mocks the hours, peering from the peppermint dappled walls. Nobody works on his beat. A brown wasted Wilton paws the floor, a mishmash of pounded mesh trails to the door. A hanging fluorescent corpse with an impediment blinks his eye. Frank heaves himself up, flattening his dishevelled grey polyester suit that he had thrown himself into. He uses the dog and bone.

Frank arrives at the scene of the crime. A three-bedroomed ticky-tacky terraced house, which the council knocked up in the fifties. He plods down the concrete cancerous path pointing to a green peeling door. The alabaster lace twitches.

The croupier enters, holding up his ace warrant card with pride. The brittle Barbara Cartland of eighty years, dressed in pinks and pearls, sits silently, not showing her hand. Her manacled sons, still attached by their umbilical cords, hover around their mum with no sign of emotion. Gladys cocks her head to one side. Her left lower lip droops for effect. She dribbles drivel about finding Bill dead in the morning by his bed.

Frank clocks the sons. One, a slim shifty silent type; the other, a bumbling guy with startled bleached hair and baby-blue eyes. Both poorly dressed, which rings alarm bells. They are playing the parts of being devoted sons, but they knew what was in it for them as their mother succeeded their stepfather. Frank has seen strange stories play out before him where money is concerned.

"Which one of you is Ian?" Frank asks.

"I am," replies the obese one of the two.

"Why did you give a statement to the police officer? It should have just been your mother."

"The young police officer took two statements. I tried to help Mum to remember, as she was confused. Firstly, she told me Bill, who wasn't well, had fallen out of the bed, and then she said he had fallen down the stairs," quivers Ian.

Frank scribbles frantically in his dog-eared notebook. Without raising his eyes, he makes a call to collect more information from other family members and retreats.

Frank lights up another fag in his car. He reclines, surrounded by discarded food wrappings and empty open-mouthed fag packets, screaming 'Smoking Kills'. He slowly draws on his cigarette, savouring the second, and exhales. The grey smog crawls up his face. The gasping engine of the car splutters to life and Frank speeds away in his Cortina. Next stop: to see the dead man's offspring.

The door of the grand Cotswold home is opened by a smart woman called Jenny. *Not short of a bob or two here*, thinks Frank. Sprawled in the lounge on the Regency striped sofa is Dave, the younger sibling. Frank notes his frayed jeans and jaded T-shirt emblazoned with 'Ark at Ee'. Dave cracks his fingers and fidgets. His legs twitch uncontrollably on their invisible strings. Frank realises a slug of booze would dampen Dave's nerves.

Veiled in domesticity, Jenny fluffs in her nesting box and makes Frank a cup of tea (he desperately wants another cigarette but dare not smoke in her lounge). He asks Dave for his recollections. Frank listens intently to Dave's tale of events.

"I got a call from Gladys eight o'clock on Sunday morning, saying she couldn't wake up Dad who was on the floor. I told her to phone 999. I arrived at Dad's house fifteen minutes later. Gladys hadn't bothered to call the ambulance or the police. I did, but it was too late."

Frank slides his nicotine-stained fingers through his thinning hair and clears his throat. Jenny's façade crumbles, her eyes cup the silent tears, her upper lip quivers slightly. "Dad was stiff, his open mouth frozen with shock. The police hid the rest of his body from me with a blanket before I was allowed to go into the bedroom. He was like the painting of 'The Scream' with false teeth in." Frank is welded to the conversation. "His whistler was in his ear as well," wheezes Dave. "He lived across the road from the White Lion and was glad he couldn't hear chucking out time when he took his hearing aid out to sleep. It was odd he still had it in – and his teeth?"

In unison, Frank and Dave clear their choking phlegm. Frank's eyes ping-pong across the room.

"Shall I carry on?" asks Jenny. Frank nods. "Gladys and Dad were rowing the night before Dad's death. I heard them on my answerphone. I wish I hadn't deleted the call. They were leaving a message saying they weren't coming in the morning for their usual coffee, and Gladys was yelling at Dad to put the phone down."

"Does your father drive to your house?"

"Yes," Jenny continues. "When I arrived at the house the following morning, Dave told me Dad was dead. I rushed to comfort Gladys, who looked surprisingly unmoved and was dressed. To let Dave in, she must have stood on a chair to unbolt the top lock. She supposedly couldn't walk and was unstable without her heavy sticks, so this was strange. The lounge was sprayed with blood. Gladys needed the toilet, so I helped her upstairs. I noticed blood up the stairs and spots on the lounge door. There were also pools of blood on the windowsills. Nothing made sense. Gladys' emotionally retarded sons appeared and stood in silence, not attempting to comfort their mother or help to clear up the blood. I busied around with cloth in hand to wipe as much of Dad's blood from the surfaces, checking with the police if it was alright to do so."

Frank pricks his ears up. He clears his throat once again and reaches into his pocket for his putcher to catch his mucus eels.

"I want the telephone calls checked the night before Dad's death from their landline," Jenny begs.

"Fine," replies Frank.

Frank makes his way back to the office, which is a grey stone affair covered in snatches and grabs of graffiti (not Banksy's) just off Nelson Street, in the heart of Bristol. He eases himself out of the car. The magnetic force of the Red

Bull opposite draws him in through the cheerless rays of the afternoon sun. He pauses in the doorway and lights up another fix, takes a few heavy desperate drags and carelessly flicks the butt away.

The pub has seen better days. A stagnant musty stench of stale beer and damp mingle with the acrid aroma of toilets. Sticky tables covered in faecal-ringed mats and back-breaking chairs rest on a gloopy Axminster, which delights in sucking the squelching shoes. Rows of pewter tankards droop dejectedly from the ceiling, staring through a mist of dust.

"Hi, Frank," says creepy Colin.

The slightly sweating, middle-aged primate poser stalks the bar. His rolled shirtsleeves hug his elbows, exposing his hirsute tattooed dragging arms.

"Starting early today, Frank. What's your poison?"

"A pint of Courage Best, please, mate. Alcohol makes the world a kinder place."

Frank downs the frothing pint, with a chalked isogloss mapping the upper lip, to the piped music of 'Won't Go Quietly' by Example and scuttles off to the office.

Frank's hunch pays off. After an hour, he finds a file on the thin shifty hound from Hades. He ran a massage parlour and brothel near a secondary school in the East End of London. He has done time. That's why John could not make eye contact; he had history.

The phone rings. Jenny is flustered. "This might be irrelevant, Inspector, but a few months before Dad died, he arrived at my house and was in pain retrieving his arm from his jacket.

He told me he'd taken a tumble in the garden. Two weeks later, he had two black eyes and a small scar across the bridge of his nose. He said he had bumped into a door."

"What's this leading to?"

"I don't know," says Jenny. "Sorry I bothered you." She hangs up, too worried to reveal the horrible thoughts that are keeping her awake at night.

Days later, Frank, who feeds on facts not predetermined guesses, is following up on all leads. The landlines in Gladys' house are checked, but did she have a mobile? Jenny's daughter swore she did. Gladys snapped that no, she didn't. The funeral is allowed to take place and the inquest would be held in due course.

All are summoned to Jenny and Dave's childhood home in Oak Drive, Avonmouth, for the funeral arrangements.

"Which favourite suit would you like the deceased to be buried in?" asks the vicar, innocently.

Gladys replies, "Bury him in a shroud. They are blue – blue was his favourite colour."

"Did I hear you right?" snaps a shocked Dave.

Gladys' eyes flash with danger. The room closes in. Jenny and Dave immediately knew they were going to be stamped out on the decision-making as Gladys was his wife. She also doesn't want to pay for any service sheets for the funeral with Bill's photo on.

The funeral is a stark affair. A few loyal stragglers from Bill's bowling club show their faces. The flittermouse arrives in a wheelchair, flanked by her black vampires, who hang by her side. The rancid reel, wrapped up in herself, has never used a wheelchair before. She wants the sympathy vote. Everyone at the funeral is fooled by Gladys' fabricated flimflam of frailty.

Jenny waits with bated breath for flashes of lightning to strike Gladys and the church crosses to spin. Jenny and Dave cling to each other, the blood ties stronger than ever.

Jenny and Dave meet with Frank again.

Jenny tells him, "We went to see Gladys. We were told Dad hadn't left a will. Although Dad lived frugally with Gladys for thirty-five years after Mum left him, he recently received considerable inheritance money from his cousin. We asked if we could have one last look in his bedroom. There were drawers choked with paperwork, sealed in clear plastic bags. I found a framed photo of Dad and I discarded on top of his wardrobe. Why? Was it Gladys who threw it up there in jealousy or did Dad throw it up there so the witch was happy? A woman always knows the hiles of a woman better than any man."

"I wanted his bowling bag," mumbles Dave, wanting any little memento of his dad. His palms sweat. A rash snakes across his neck. Panting, he reaches into his pocket for his blue plastic inhaler and takes two puffs. He wishes he could have a swift drink.

Jenny jogs her memory and recalls what Ian's wife had said quietly at the funeral to Dave: "Whatever has she done to her husband this time?"

Dave realises that even though him and his sister have been kept at a distance, the one thing they had was his dad's ashes. He signed the papers at the funeral directors. He is the only one who can remove them. Frank tells him to take control of his dead father's ashes, to man up and do what he needs to do. After all, Gladys could scream and shout for a few weeks, but it would all be over soon.

"What the hell are we doing here?"

"Don't blaspheme in a graveyard," Jenny replies. She reaches into her handbag and retrieves a sheet of paper. Sobs explode through a plethora of words, "Do not stand at my grave and weep…"

On a bleak December morning in Dunster, Somerset, two leaded soldiers stand to attention, swallowed up in grief. The sympathetic needles of rain polish the face of the Bristol Channel with tears. Jenny and Dave scatter the blanket of ashes of their father over the sodden granite graves of their grandmother and grandfather, knowing in their hearts it is where their dad would want to rest. His sister is also in the next grave.

Later the following week, only Jenny, Dave and Jenny's daughter turn up at the coroner's court for the inquest. The contradictory statements are read out.

"We do not have sufficient evidence to prosecute, therefore the verdict is Accidental Death," announces the coroner.

The assistant shakes his head in disbelief. The coroner apologises to the three family members after the court case, but apparently there is not enough evidence to prosecute and no one would ever know what really happened that night.

On his final day at the grubby office, Frank lights up another cigarette. He remembers that Ian said Bill was not a well man. Ian was lying. Frank had done his paperwork. Bill's doctor told him William had a medical two weeks before he died and was healthy for his age, bowling three times a week. Frank knew he was still driving his car over to Jenny's every week for coffee. Bill was unbelievably fit, but where did he get all his bruising over several weeks, and what happened on the night of his death to produce that amount of blood all over the house? Nothing made sense.

Did the young police officer, being his first week at work, take all the necessary information down correctly when taking the wife and stepson's statements. Frank thought he should have been in short trousers he was so young.

The tough old weather-beaten cop feels niggled. He taps his desk over and over again. Something is missing. Bill might have been old, but Frank won't dismiss him because of his age.

Undeterred, Frank makes one last phone call and, like a Jack Russell that has spotted a rabbit, makes a dash.

He rings the rusty doorbell of the old lady's house and Gladys calls out, "The door is ajar. Come on in, dear."

She is sat centre stage, still playing the frail old lady leading role with her hands hugging her head.

"Sorry to bother you, madam, but I have a few questions

I want clarified, as I am still not happy about your husband's death."

"First of all, my dear," Gladys trills, "could you pass me my glasses on the floor? I think they're by the side of my armchair. I'm finding it difficult to get up at my age."

Frank's knees creak as he bends down to feel around the chair.

In the corner of the room, destiny awaits. With pinprick eyes, the heartless black widow looks down on her prey caught in the spun web of her salivated lies. She silently slides her crooked claw under the settee and grasps her weighty bloodstained walking stick.

Frank could remember no more!

WEEP, DEAR WILLOW, LIKE ME

Wave upon wave in grief,
She weeps in her own solitary space,
Amongst the brutal striking hands of time.
She rises and falls like the tide,
In an attempt to whip away,
The memories of an unrequited love.
Octopus tentacles twist and curl,
Amongst tear-stained tissues of cloud.
Her tussled majestic mane unravels.
She beats her broken wings,
Against the harsh keys of the wind,
Soaking up the sadness of the sky.
Trapped within her own isolation,
She battles in an attempt to free her sprit.
In torment, the enchantress giddily spins,
Like a carousel,
Whilst her roots tenaciously search,
For the soothing stream of love.

PANTOUM

WHAT IF? IS THE QUESTION

He sits motionless in a moment of great calm, knowing only God has the key.
He wishes to ask tangled questions, of which he already knows the answers.
From his dark space, what if he thinks outside of the box marked with 'C'.
A frozen smile that holds negativity forces its way across the specialist's face.

He wishes to ask tangled questions, of which he already knows the answers.
In the language of life's blows, he hears the silent echo of an Amen.
A frozen smile that holds negativity forces its way across the specialist's face.
My love waits patiently in death's shadow, awaiting answers, and shivers.

In the language of life's blows, he hears the silent echo of an Amen.
Through a buttress of clouds, the future marches to his door and turns away.
My love waits patiently in death's shadow, awaiting answers, and shivers.
Although speech is shallow, he awaits words of hope to nail to the walls.

Through a buttress of clouds, the future marches to his door and turns away.
He sits motionless in a moment of great calm, knowing only God has the key.
Although speech is shallow, he awaits words of hope to nail to the walls.
From his dark space, what if he thinks outside of the box marked with 'C'.

WHO OVERFILLED MY BUCKET?

Who overfilled my bucket?
With flea-coloured puce,
Of pugnacious juice.
Who overfilled my bucket?

Who overfilled my bucket?
With a bubbling foaming floss,
Of egotistical tear-stained dross.
Who overfilled my bucket?

Who overfilled my bucket?
With waves of greed that rock the tin,
My hopes as rusty as the rim.
Who overfilled my bucket?

Who overfilled my bucket?
There is a tiny festering hole,
Dripping segments of my dying soul.
Who overfilled my bucket?

Who overfilled my bucket?
Hope in the mullock of my mind,
In heaviness is treading time.
Who overfilled my bucket?

Who overfilled my bucket?
My childhood was so stained with pain,
My mind it really needs to change.
Who overfilled my bucket?

Who overfilled my bucket?
It's filled to the brim with past decay,
There's nothing more for me to say.
Who overfilled my bucket?

Who overfilled my bucket?
It's me! Oh, fuck it!

WITHIN THE SEASONS OF MY WEATHERED SOUL.

Lost in balkanised segments,
Of my debased darkness,
In my hopelessness to un-clump,
I amputate to stumps,
Thoughts too weighty, I need to dump.
Daggy me, in my futility
I have the inability,
to realise the brittleness of truth.
I ink out mind's memoirs of sadness,
and momentary madness,
from the thin sheets of tissues,
Of unresolved issues.
I drown in a SPRING tide of self-pity,
As banshee spirits yell,
In the torment of life's swell.
I await the sudden rush of love,
To flow towards my heart space,
Alas the SUMMER sun drops like a stone,
Upon the menacing mantle,
Of my gethsemane making,
Shadowing the unvarnished me.
I endeavour to reap the AUTUMN harvest,

Of a quiet eye,
But WINTER'S frost of my past,
Still comes and goes.
Constellations of unfulfilled promises,
Gather like dust, and rust,
On my screwed winch of woes.
My third blind eye,
Rolls itself across my moodiness,
And in dimness this virago fails to see,
Her own self-inflicted misery.
I am a disconsolate disconnected soul,
That flounders, boat-like, in a jagged squall.
Battering myself like a ram,
Against the bars of my ribcage,
This beating heart's wild waters,
And winds prevail.
The milk of kindness, to not much avail,
Flows in another direction.
Love refusing to enter,
Turns its face away,
At my imperfections.
I look inwards at a conditioned me,
That cannot change.
Trapped in shallows,
Of my own opinions,
I travel aimlessly,
Searching for daylight,
Within the seasons of my weathered soul.

SUITCASES

Waiting patiently on aged paint peeled wooden trolleys,
For the arrival of the 11.10,
Faded leather suitcases, phantoms of hope,
Stacked one on top of the other,
Devour the station with expectations,
Of far-off destinations.

Frayed straps, battered bodies and broken brass clasps,
Hold their secrets hostage.
They await in the mocking drizzle,
Listening intently for the panting breath,
Of their hissing, swearing saviour,
As he snakes his way around the distant bend.

The monster, avoiding the occasional land slip,
Grinds to a halt, announcing plosive consonants,
At the annoyance of his late arrival.
The brakes squeal upon the metal tracks.
Another broth of smoke-filled breath bursts forth,
Leaving its cloud of antagonism in the drizzled air.

A porter saunters down the empty station,
In his gloomy well-worn faded uniform,
And takes control of the soiled trolly.
The closed mouthed suitcases silently sigh,
As amongst the motes of dust and the brief day's light,
They know their freedom is guaranteed.

This book is printed on paper from sustainable sources managed under the Forest Stewardship Council (FSC) scheme.

It has been printed in the UK to reduce transportation miles and their impact upon the environment.

For every new title that Troubador publishes, we plant a tree to offset CO_2, partnering with the More Trees scheme.

For more about how Troubador offsets its environmental impact, see www.troubador.co.uk/sustainability-and-community

A Plethora of Poetry and Prose

A Plethora of Poetry and Prose

Julie Nancy Wiltshire

Copyright © 2025 Julie Nancy Wiltshire
Illustrations by Maria Over

The moral right of the author has been asserted.

Apart from any fair dealing for the purposes of research or private study, or criticism or review, as permitted under the Copyright, Designs and Patents Act 1988, this publication may only be reproduced, stored or transmitted, in any form or by any means, with the prior permission in writing of the publishers, or in the case of reprographic reproduction in accordance with the terms of licences issued by the Copyright Licensing Agency. Enquiries concerning reproduction outside those terms should be sent to the publishers.

The manufacturer's authorised representative in the EU
for product safety is Authorised Rep Compliance Ltd,
71 Lower Baggot Street, Dublin D02 P593 Ireland (www.arccompliance.com)

Troubador Publishing Ltd
Unit E2 Airfield Business Park,
Harrison Road, Market Harborough,
Leicestershire. LE16 7UL
Tel: 0116 2792299
Email: books@troubador.co.uk
Web: www.troubador.co.uk

ISBN 978-1-83628-329-4

British Library Cataloguing in Publication Data.
A catalogue record for this book is available from the British Library.

Printed and bound by CPI Group (UK) Ltd, Croydon, CR0 4YY
Typeset in 11pt Adobe Garamond Pro by Troubador Publishing Ltd, Leicester, UK

Dedicated to all my family and friends.

Contents

A BRIDGE TOO FAR
A CACOPHONY OF SOUND
A DAY AT THE SEASIDE
A DUSTING OF DEATH
A LEAF IN THE CHAPTER OF WAR
A PEACEFUL SATISFACTION
A SNOWY CHRISTMAS
ABORTION
ADDICTION
AGED MOLE
ALONG THE BRUTAL SHORES OF MY WORLD
AMID THE WINTER SNOW
AN UNWANTED VISITOR
AS THE STARS BLOW OUT OF THE SKY
BEIGE JACKETS
BELLY DANCING IN BIRKENHEAD
BIRD BROOCH
BLINDED BY NORMALITY
BOB
BRIZZLE BLUES

CAMERA CRAZY
CAN I BEGIN ANEW?
CANCER THE CRAB
   (KNOW THYSELF)
COBWEB
CONCRETE COFFIN
COSTA COFFEE
DARK DEEDS
DENT DE LION
DIAMOND IN THE SKY
DON'T WALK IN MY SHOES
ENSANGUINING OUR HEAVY
   HEARTS
ENVIRONMENTAL RAPE
FLY FISHING
FORGIVENESS
FREEDOM OF THE FALL
FUNNEL TO THE FUTURE
GALLOPING TO MY GRAVE
GRANDCHILDREN
HAIR
HELL HATH NO FURY
HIDDEN WITHIN MYSELF
HIDE AND SEEK
HOLDING FATE IN THE PALM OF HER
   HAND